Transferable Concepts For

Powerful
Living

Transferable Concepts For

Powerful Living

Bill Bright

TRANSFERABLE CONCEPTS FOR POWERFUL LIVING
by Bill Bright

Published by
HERE'S LIFE PUBLISHERS, INC.
P.O. Box 1576
San Bernardino, CA 92402

HLP Product No. 403386
© 1985, Campus Crusade for Christ
All rights reserved.
Printed in the United States of America.

Except where otherwise indicated, all Scripture quotations in this book are taken from the New American Standard Bible, © The Lockman Foundation 1960, 1962, 1963, 1968, 1971,1972,1973, 1975. Used by permission. Other Scripture quotations are from *The Living Bible* (TLB), © 1971 by Tyndale House Publishers, Wheaton Illinois, and used by permission; and from the King James Version (KJV).

Library of Congress Cataloging-in-Publication Data

Bright, Bill.
    Transferable concepts for powerful living.
    Abridged ed. of: Handbook of concepts for living.
© 1981.
    1. Theology, Doctrinal — Popular works. 2. Witness bearing (Christianity) 3. Evangelistic work.
4. Christian Life — 1960   I. Bright, Bill.
Handbook of concepts for living. II. Title.
BT77.B772   1985   248.4   85-80372
ISBN 0-86605-163-5 (pbk.)

FOR MORE INFORMATION, WRITE:

L.I.F.E. — P.O. Box A399, Sydney South 2000, Australia
Campus Crusade for Christ of Canada — Box 300, Vancouver, B.C., V6C 2X3, Canada
Campus Crusade for Christ — 103 Friar Street, Reading RG1 1EP, Berkshire, England
Lay Institute for Evangelism — P.O. Box 8786, Auckland 3, New Zealand
Great Commission Movement of Nigeria — P.O. Box 500, Jos, Plateau State Nigeria, West Africa
Life Ministry — P.O. Box/Bus 91015, Auckland Park 2006, Republic of South Africa
Campus Crusade for Christ International — Arrowhead Springs, San Bernardino, CA 92414, U.S.A.

ACKNOWLEDGMENTS

We are indebted to Carolyn Phillips for her adaptation of the Transferable Concepts in this present format.

CONTENTS

CHAPTER ONE

HOW TO BE SURE
YOU ARE A CHRISTIAN

The young man beside me thanked God for coming into his life, then closed his prayer. But as we stood to our feet something still seemed to be troubling him. "It's probably not important," he said when I asked. "It's just that, well, somehow I thought I'd *feel different*, but I don't. Maybe God didn't hear my prayer. . . ." Then he asked a question heard so often, "How can I be *sure* I am a Christian?"

This is a question that arises in the hearts of people around the world, from every walk of life. It's a question that troubles even pastors and involved lay workers. The question demands an answer.

— A Pastor, a faithful minister for over forty years, admitted that he was not sure of his own salvation, though he had led countless people to Christ.

— The wife of a dedicated evangelist sat weeping in my office. "My husband and I have introduced thousands of people to Christ in the thirty years of our ministry," she said, "but I have never been sure of my own salvation." She twisted the tissue in her hands. "I've never admitted this to anyone before, but I'm desperate! *I have to know that I'm saved.*"

It occurs to me that you, like these sincere people, also may be haunted by questions about God. You may wonder, *can I really know God?* Maybe you've been raised with an exposure to the teachings of Jesus, and have been familiar with His claims and His love since early childhood. You may have believed in God and His Son for years, yet you struggle. Are you convinced that you would spend eternity with Him if you should die today?

Or perhaps you have only recently received Christ and are still not sure that "anything happened." Your life seems to be the same as before, and you have serious misgivings about the reality of your decision to trust Christ. You find yourself questioning the reality of salvation.

It is also possible that you are among a large group of people still looking for a way to make God a part of your life. You may long to be certain that you will spend eternity with Him. You may need the confidence that assurance of your salvation could bring.

Successful people in business, Christian workers, students, pillars of the church . . . all of us have the right to an assurance of our salvation. Why does this fearful uncertainty exist among so many who genuinely want to know God, even among those who have sought and served Him for years?

To a large degree, the fault lies in being poorly grounded or having mistaken information about who God is. The confusion in sincere hearts often revolves around the true meaning of Christ's crucifixion and resurrection and what is required to received Jesus Christ as Savior.

If any of these doubts sound like your own, the moments you spend reading the rest of this chapter could be the best investment of time that you *ever* make. Come with me once and for all through the steps to assurance.

First, understand that becoming a Christian means that we accept God's gift of love and forgiveness through His Son Jesus Christ. It is the greatest gift ever offered to man, and it is free to anyone who accepts it. It has the power to change lives. It bears with it the promise of eternity with God. It is a personal relationship with Jesus Christ, the Son of God Himself.

This commitment is not unlike the decision to marry. Although the love of a young couple is undeniably filled with great emotion, the decision to marry is a threefold process involving the intellect, the emotions, and the will.

Love between two people often comes quickly and easily. But the intellect becomes involved at the moment they begin to entertain thoughts about marriage. They must try to decide whether the one they love is a "good choice" for a life-partner. There are many unemotional decisions they must make and the final decision — to leave all others and cleave to each other — is made as an act of the will. They testify to that decision when they say "I do" and become husband and wife.

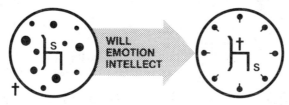

Becoming a Christian is a decision, a choice that involves our *intellect, emotions* and *will.* Though valid, it is not enough to believe intellectually in Christ, nor is it enough to have an emotional experience, no matter how life-changing it may seem. Becoming a Christian is an act of the will, a clear-cut decision to receive Christ into our lives as Savior and Lord.

Intellectual Understanding

Being certain of your decision to become a Christian requires a clear grasp of what is involved in making the choice. It demands an *intellectual understanding* of God's promises and who He is. It is not a "blind leap of faith," as some would label it. On the contrary, Christianity is built upon historical fact, documented by centuries of investigation by world-renowned scholars. As a result, we have more historical evidence to document the events of Jesus of Nazareth, than we have to prove the defeat of Napoleon at Waterloo.

Historian and author, Kenneth Scott Latourette, director of the department of religion at the graduate school of Yale University, said, in reference to Jesus Christ, "Measured by its fruits in the human race, that short life has been the most influential ever lived on this planet. As we have been at pains to point out, the impress of that life, far from fading with the passing centuries, has deepened. Through Him millions of individuals have been transformed and have begun to live the kind of life which He exemplified. Gauged by the consequences which have followed, the birth, life, death and resurrection of Jesus have been the most important events in the history of man. Measured by His influence, Jesus is central in the human story."

The British scholar, W. H. Griffith Thomas, said, "The testimony to the present work of Jesus Christ is no less real today than it has been in the past. In the case of all the other great names of the world's history, the inevitable and invariable experience has been that the particular man is first a power, then only a name, and last of all a mere memory. Of Jesus Christ the exact opposite is true. He died on a cross of shame, His name gradually became more and more powerful, and He is the greatest influence in the world today."

George Romanes, British physicist, says, "It is on all sides worth considering (blatant ignorance or base vulgarity alone excepted) that the revolution effected by Christianity in human life is immeasurable and unparalleled by any other movement in history."

Hundreds of years before Jesus' birth, Scripture recorded the words of the great prophets of Israel foretelling His coming. The Old Testament, written by many individuals over a period of 1,500 years, contains more than 300 references to His coming. The New Testament records the words of Jesus Himself, claiming to be God. "I and the Father are one," He said. "He who has seen Me has seen the Father" (John 10:30; 14:9).

To become a Christian it is necessary to face the claims of the Savior, weigh them intellectually, and choose to accept the truth that the evidence points to: Jesus is God. He died willingly for your sins and mine; He was buried, and rose again after three days; He is alive now and wants to come into your life and be your Savior and Lord. It is your choice. *You must decide* what *you* will do with the claims of Christ.

Emotional Involvement

Involvement of the *emotions* is a part of being a Christian. Emotions are nothing more than feelings or reactions to an act, event or experience which occurs in our lives. But we often misunderstand or misinterpret feelings and end up frustrated and confounded. For many people the emotional element of Christianity has caused great confusion concerning assurance of salvation.

The emotional tenor of another Christian's life does not always match our own. Too often we are guilty of comparisons. They tend to leave us doubting the depth of our salvation and sincerity of our commitment. The truth is that no two people are alike and, therefore, cannot be expected to respond to the experiences of their faith in the same way. One may respond to his Christian experience in a highly emotional, visible manner, while another may respond just as deeply to the same experience, but deal with it within himself, quietly, privately. Is one response "better" than the other? Is it possible to judge? Is it even necessary?

The Scriptures record life-changing experiences that occurred in the lives of real people. One passage (Acts 9:1-19) reveals the colorful character of the man called Paul, a fiery-tempered zealot who actively threw himself into the causes he believed in. When God confronted Paul, he was in the midst of a campaign to literally kill off all the Christians he could find. God's method of dealing with Paul was tempered for his specific emotional needs. God spoke aloud, using dramatic circumstances to assure Paul's undivided attention. He captured him completely, and held him fast until he had heard in his heart what God was saying to him. Paul responded to the message, but remained emotionally the same. He was still zealous and enthusiastic in his involvements, but God had given him a new direction. Instead of using his energies to destroy the church of Christ, he was now spreading the gospel with conviction.

Timothy, on the other hand, comes across as a steady, quiet, faithful supporter of the cause of Christ. He had been raised by a Christian mother and grand-mother, and his faith had formed early, gradually as he grew to manhood. He heard no commands from heaven. It was not necessary for him to experience what Paul did in order to hear God's voice. God seemed to speak in whispers to Timothy, and his tender heart missed very little of what was directed toward him.

The lives of Paul and Timothy were used greatly to spread the seeds of Christianity to the uttermost parts of the world, and they clearly demonstrate the fact that God does not speak to all of us in the same way. He communicates with each of us *in ways tailored to our specific needs*, to incorporate our strengths and make strong our weaknesses. Seeking an emotional experience or condemning its lack in another's life, or judging a brother or sister in Christ as "too emotional" or "too conservative," has no place in the life of a Christian committed to spiritual growth. Emotions are a valid part of the Christian life but they are fickle, often changing like the weather. We need to base our faith on *more* than emotions. It cannot be our only gauge. The assurance of our salvation is based on:

> the trustworthiness of God;
> the confirmation of the Holy Spirit; and
> the evidence of a changed life.

First, we must base our salvation on *the external witness of the Word of God*. It is the authority of the very Word of God that provides a solid foundation for our faith in Him. To those of us who believe, the promises are there (John 1:12).

"We believe men who witness in our courts, and so surely we can believe whatever God declares. And God declares that Jesus is his Son. All who believe this know in their hearts that it is true. If anyone doesn't believe this, he is actually calling God a liar, because he doesn't believe what God has said about his Son. And what is it that God has said? That he has given us eternal life, and that this life is in his Son. So whoever has God's Son has life; whoever does not have his Son does not have life. I have written this to you who believe in the Son of God so that you may know you have eternal life" (1 John 5:9-13, TLB). *There is assurance in God's Word.*

Second, there is *the internal witness of the Holy Spirit*. Paul wrote to the Romans, "For his Holy Spirit speaks to us deep in our hearts, and tells us that we really are God's children" (Romans. 8:16, TLB). It was such an important point that he emphasized it again when he wrote to the Christians in Thessalonica. "For when we brought you the Good News," he writes, "it was not just meaningless chatter to you; no, you listened with great interest. What we told you produced a powerful effect upon you, for the Holy Spirit gave you great and full assurance that what we said was true" (1 Thessalonians 1:5a, TLB). *There is assurance because of the Holy Spirit.*

The third proof that we have experienced a new birth and have become children of the living God, lies in the evidence of *changed lives:* ours and those of other Christians around us. In Paul's letter to the Thessalonian Christians, he adds, "Our very lives were further proof to you of the truth of our message. So you became our followers and the Lord's; for you received our message with joy from the Holy Spirit in spite of the trials and sorrows it brought you. Then you yourselves became an example to all the other Christians in Greece. And now the Word of the Lord has spread out from you to others everywhere, far beyond your boundaries, for wherever we go we find people telling us about your remarkable faith in God" (1 Thessalonians 1:5b-8, TLB).

Later, Paul writes to Colossian Christians and says, "The same Good News that came to you is going out all over the world and changing lives everywhere, just as it changed yours that very first day you heard it and understood about God's great kindness to sinners" (Colossians 1:6, TLB).

"And how can we be sure that we belong to him?" the apostle John asks, then answers, "By looking within ourselves: are we really trying to do what he wants us to? Someone may say, 'I am a Christian; I am on my way to heaven; I belong to Christ.' But if he doesn't do what Christ tells him to, he is a liar. But those who do what Christ tells them to will learn to love God more and more. *That is the way to know whether or not you are a Christian.* Anyone who says he is a Christian should live as Christ did" (1 John 2:3-6, TLB, italics ours).

The genuine desire within us to obey God and live as Christ did is confirmation that we have been born again. With time our lives will change to demonstrate to others the new life within us. Jesus said, "I will only reveal myself to those who love me and obey me. The Father will love them too, and we will come to them and live with them. Anyone who doesn't obey me doesn't love me. And remember, I am not making up this answer to your question! It is the answer given by the Father who sent me" (John 14:23-24, TLB). If a strong desire to please the Lord Jesus with our obedience is missing from our lives, we have reason to question the authenticity of our salvation. *There is assurance in a changed life.*

We have seen that emotions are a valid, important part of life, including their role in the Christian experience. But the assurance of our faith requires more than just "feeling saved." We need to depend on the external witness of the Word of God, and we must be conscious of the internal witness of our salvation through the indwelling Holy Spirit. Coupled with the changes we will see in our own lives and the lives of other Christians, we have all the evidence we need of the truth of our salvation.

Involvement of the Will

Now we come to the matter of the will. It is often the will that keeps a person from a longed-for relationship with Christ.

Some time ago I visited one of our nation's most prestigious seminaries where a friend of mine was completing his doctorate. We were on our way to meet one of his favorite professors, a widely known, respected theologian and scholar who had given years of his life to train thousands of young people for the ministry. "He's a good man," my friend said. "He's warm-hearted and I like him, but he doesn't believe in the deity of Christ, or that the Bible is the Word of God." He looked at me and grinned. "I'm hoping you'll be able to say something to him to change his mind."

Almost before we had completed our greetings the professor asked, "You talk to college students in your travels, don't you, Mr. Bright?"

I nodded.

"What do you tell the ones who want to become Christians?"

I hesitated, weighing what I should say to this brilliant man. Was it an academic argument he sought? Curiosity perhaps? Before I answered he spoke again.

"Let me be more honest with you," he said. "I want to become a Christian. Can you tell me how?"

After all his years of doubting, of teaching young men and women against the deity of Christ and the inspiration of Scripture, I wondered what had made him change his mind.

"It has been a struggle for me to allow God the right to control my life. I know it's pride," he said quietly. "I've done quite well in my field; I've received coveted honors and found that I like being considered an authority in the academic world. The thought of laying that down, and humbling myself before God has been hateful to me."

He leaned against the edge of his desk, and looked out the window into the distance. "For years I have denied Scripture its rightful place as the inspired Word of God, and I have taught so many to do the same thing. But lately I've been reading the Bible with a new understanding. And I've read several of the works of the church fathers too, men used greatly of God, like John Wesley and St. Augustine. Intellectually, I am convinced that Jesus is indeed the Son of God, but I don't know Him as my Savior. Can you help me change that?"

That day, this man of international renown changed the direction of his life. He had known this was the answer he sought, but because of his will — his desire to remain in control of his life — he had kept God at arm's length.

Though the professor struggled with his pride, others who have made an intellectual decision about God, and recognize Him as who He claims to be, may put off accepting Him as Savior because they fear the consequences. Some are convinced that if they commit their lives to Jesus they will instantly be sentenced to a life of boredom and misery.

I chatted with a young man for several hours one afternoon on a large mid-western college campus. He was sure God meant to bore him to death.

"I'm an atheist," he said with a swagger, "and a confirmed party animal. I'm having the time of my life doing just as I please. If you think I'm giving all that up so I can drag around campus looking like the end of the world, you'd better think again. Christians are people my set makes jokes about. They haven't got anything I want."

But several faithful Christian friends in his fraternity continued to pray for his salvation, and within a few weeks this same young man who had been so filled with himself, invited Christ into his life. "I guess I always knew Jesus was the Son of God, but I fought Him. I was so afraid He would condemn me to a life of misery, and I love having a good time. It was that verse in Matthew 16:26 that made me begin to wonder, where it says, 'What will a man be profited, if he gains the whole world, and forfeits his soul?'

"And then one afternoon for some reason, I picked up my Bible and ran across John 10:10, where Jesus said, 'I came that they might have life, and might have it abundantly.' When I started looking at my life and asking if it was what I would call 'abundant' I had to admit it was pretty empty. Jesus has made such an incredible difference. I can hardly put it into words. But it's great!"

It is only through trusting God with our lives that we discover how much He *adds to life*. But many continue to fear He will take away the things they love. A successful coach for a pro ball team confided one morning over breakfast that for years he had been a Christian, but had always withheld committing his professional life to God. "I just knew that if I ever gave it to God," he said, "He would take it away. I was afraid He would want me to go into the ministry instead. But I *love* what I do. It *is* my life." His reputation spoke highly of him as a man of great skill and professional character. It was easy to see his love for his players and for the game.

As he sat beside me stirring his coffee, a peaceful expression slipped onto his rugged face. "You know," he said at last, "when I finally did give it *all* to God, I realized that *He wanted me in coaching.* Part of the reason I love the game is because of the skill and ability God has given me to do what I do. I am serving Him right where I am. But I never really understood until I was willing to give it up."

The human will is a powerful dimension of our ability to believe our salvation. It can keep us from trusting God fully; it can create unfounded doubts; it can invent reasons for us to allow sin in our lives, knowing that what we are doing causes pain to the heart of God.

When sin is allowed in our lives, it is not unusual for us to begin to doubt the validity of our salvation. Until our hearts are willing to admit it is sin, and deal with our disobedience, we often find ourselves creating arguments against believing God. It may seem to be "easier" than confessing our sin before Him, but only for a season.

Other times our will to believe fully in our salvation is hampered because we have been deceived by Satan. When a Christian allows willful sin in his life, he may become convinced that God will never forgive him for what he has done. It is a clever trick of the master deceiver himself, but unless the estranged believer determines to return to God and accept His forgiveness, he may condemn himself to a life of fear, wondering about his salvation, afraid he will always be separated from God because of choices he has made.

And so we see that God never keeps His children at arm's length. It is a trick of Satan. God extends assurance of His salvation to all His children, at all times, with no exception. If we are unsure of where we stand, we need to take inventory of our intellect, our emotions and our will.

To be assured of our position in Christ, we must be aware intellectually, of the basic truths:

1. God loves you and has a wonderful plan for your life.
2. Man is sinful and separated from God; thus he cannot know or experience God's love and plan for him.
3. Jesus Christ is God's only provision for man's sin. Through Him you can know and experience God's love and plan for your life.
4. You must decide to receive Jesus Christ as Savior and Lord of your life; it is then you will know and experience God's love and plan for you.

Christ promised, "Behold, I stand at the door and knock; if anyone hears My voice and opens the door, I will come in to him, and will dine with him, and he with Me" (Revelation 3:20). In John's Gospel we read, "But as many as received Him, to them He gave the right to become children of God, even to those who believe in His name" (John 1:12).

Yet, it is not enough just to believe. We must have faith, accepting His promise to enter our lives regardless of what we may feel. Ephesians 2:8,9 reminds us, "For by grace you have been saved *through faith*; and that not of yourselves, it is the gift of God; not as a result of works, that no one should boast." Once we have asked Jesus into our lives, it is not necessary to ask again. Then we must believe He has come in *as He promised*! And He has said He will never leave nor abandon His children.

Faith is a muscle that becomes strong only as we exercise it. It is the difference between thinking we are saved, and *knowing*! The choice is up to you.

RECOMMENDED ASSIGNMENTS

Chapter 1

Reflect: What questions have been on my mind about my relationship with God? Or, why am I certain I am a Christian?

Interpret: Dig into the Word with this Scripture search. Look up and record some verses to support the premise: "Becoming a Christian is a decision, a choice involving our intellect, emotions and will." (For starters, refer to text.)

INTELLECT —

EMOTIONS —

WILL —

Apply: Write a personal note to a new Christian explaining how a person can be sure he is a Christian. See how many truths you can glean from the content of this chapter, try to incorporate the highlights which really impressed you personally.
Write the note on stationery and mail it to someone needing those words of explanation and encouragement!

CHAPTER TWO
HOW TO
EXPERIENCE GOD'S LOVE
AND FORGIVENESS

There were deep lines on the young face staring out the window of the train, lines that months of reliving a regretted space in time had embedded as he had served his sentence in prison. The green rolling hills and familiar pasturelands sped past until there, in the distance, he recognized the three spires of the grainery in his hometown. A lump of terror sprung into his throat and slithered down into his stomach. He would know soon. They were just a few miles from his folk's place on the outskirts of town.

He stroked the cover of the book lying open in his lap as if to touch some remains of reality. The whole thing felt like a dream. The last three years were swaddled in a haze. How could he have done it? The shame his crime had brought his mother and father was more than anyone should have to bear. How could they ever forgive him?

And all the while the train rolled on, closer to what had once been home for him . . . before. He knew when he wrote them that he had no right but he had asked them to leave a sign if they could find it in their hearts to forgive him. Just a ribbon, hanging from the old oak tree in the backyard where his tire swing had been all these years. He only wanted to see them once more and then he intended to move on, to spare them any more shame and hurt. He would know in the next few minutes.

The palms of his hands were wet with perspiration; his mouth was dry, and as much as he longed to know, he could not make himself look out the window. What would he do if the ribbon was not there?

"You all right, son?" The passenger next to him could not help but notice the young man's tension. "Something I can do for you?"

"Yes, sir, there is," he said. "Just past that bend is a big old oak tree and . . . well, I know it sounds a little strange, but would you tell me if you see a yellow ribbon in the tree somewhere? I . . . I just can't bring myself to look."

The man nodded and as the train rounded the bend he began to smile. "Is it there?" the young man asked. "Can you see the ribbon?"

"You'll have to look for yourself, son," the man said. "You wouldn't believe mé if I told you."

The young man slowly raised his head and stared in grateful disbelief. The oak tree had blossomed into a bouquet of yellow ribbons flying in the breeze from every branch. And against the fence, a man and a woman waved at the passing train carrying the son they loved.

There are Christians who, like this young man, live fearful lives, missing that sparklè, that special dynamic they had expected from Christianity. They don't smile. They scowl. They struggle. Burdens overwhelm them. *Where is the peace Jesus promised?* they wonder. What they really need is a renewed perspective of the forgiveness that is ours in Christ.

These believers are painfully aware that something is missing in their lives. Their Christianity reflects a

self-inflicted boredom. These people do not need scold-
ing from well-meaning Christian brothers and sisters.
They do not need to be convinced that life is empty
and unfulfilling. What they do need is to tap into their
spiritual resources — like love, peace and forgiveness —
the missing ingredients their salvation can bring to everyday lives. This is their rightful inheritance, available
to every believer.

Like the young man who saw the yellow ribbons,
these destitute believers simply need to understand how
to reach out and *possess* what is theirs and to discover
that the secret for knowing and experiencing forgiveness
lies in being filled with God's Spirit.

But what do we tell someone whose Christianity
is colorless? What if *you* were struggling to find the love
that eluded you as a believer. Would it really be possible
for another Christian to present profound truths clearly
enough for you to grasp and apply them in your own life?

Can one believer teach another how to experience
Christ's limitless forgiveness for themselves? The answer
is yes. Throughout our walk with Christ we repeatedly
find rewarding benefits in practicing this concept.

Paul deals with this very topic in 1 Corinthians 2
and 3. He explains why some believers lack joy and
the power of the Holy Spirit in their lives when he
writes about *the natural man, the spiritual man, and
the carnal man.*

The natural man is one who depends on his own
resources. This person says, "I'll do it my way." He is
not a Christian, and therefore cannot truly grasp the
truths of God's Word. He is self-sufficient. His interests
and ambitions are worldly and self-centered. Though
he may appear to have his act together, spiritually he
is dead — our only birthright until we invite Jesus into
our lives.

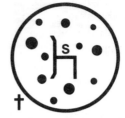

SELF-DIRECTED LIFE
S · Self is on the throne
† · Christ is outside the life
• · Interests are directed
    by self, often resulting in
    discord and frustration

The spiritual man is one who is born again into life everlasting. This person says, "I cannot make it on my own. I admit that I need God." He is indwelt and guided by the Holy Spirit, who makes it possible for him to understand the truths of God's Word. *The spiritual man is alive!* He has a vital relationship with the Lord. And because he is a channel of the Holy Spirit's power, he is constantly bearing fruit.

CHRIST-DIRECTED LIFE
† · Christ is in the life
    and on the throne
S · Self is yielding to Christ
• · Interests are directed
    by Christ, resulting in
    harmony with God's plan

The main topic of this chapter is *the carnal man.* Though he is born again, he has not tapped into the rich inheritance of his heavenly Father. Instead, he continues to live like a condemned man. He often *looks* as if all is well. He may teach Sunday school, pastor a church, or give years of his life in some remote mission field leading others to Christ. But it is a cover-up.

The bottom-line reality is that a carnal man is defeated. If he is honest, he will admit that his Christianity lacks real joy. He is constantly frustrated. In desperation he valiantly tries to live a life pleasing to God, but instead of drawing on the source of power, the Holy Spirit, he relies on his own energy and creativity for the strength he needs, and he runs into problems.

Other things reflect the carnal man's lifestyle. He

may attempt to hold tightly to God, but simultaneously refuse to loosen his grasp on material, earthly things. He finds himself possessed by his possessions. At the same time, he tries to tune-in to spiritual matters. Jesus Himself said it is impossible to serve two masters. Though the carnal man sincerely tries to please God, he is spinning his spiritual wheels. Romans 8:7 explains why: "The old sinful nature within us is against God. It never did obey God's laws and it never will" (TLB).

The sad thing is that this person never allows the Holy Spirit to mold him into the person God created him to be. Paul said in Romans 5:1,2, that we can be what God wants us to be: "So now, since we have been made right in God's sight by faith in his promises, we can have real peace with him because of what Jesus Christ our Lord has done for us. For because of our faith, he has brought us into this place of highest privilege where we now stand, and we confidently and joyfully look forward to actually becoming all that God has had in mind for us to be" (TLB).

Tremendous freedom comes wrapped up in this truth! It is our *faith in God* that pleases Him, never our efforts, despite our courageous attempts or heartfelt sincerity. Our only hope for victory over this carnal tendency, is trusting Christ to live His resurrection life in and through us. His forgiveness becomes ours when we become His children. We only need to accept it — a fact the carnal man does not comprehend.

The carnal man may not cling to his own strength simply by choice. It's possible that he suffers from a lack of accurate information, or he may be confused about who God really is and what He can do in a person's life.

SELF-DIRECTED LIFE
S · Self is on the throne
† · Christ dethroned and not allowed to direct the life
• · Interests are directed by self, often resulting in discord and frustration

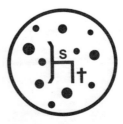

Consider the story of a poor immigrant who once bought passage on a ship to the United States. He had only enough money left over to buy a few crackers and a small block of cheese which he rationed carefully over the first few days of the voyage. But his hunger grew. He watched the ship's waiters dashing past him, carrying trays of succulent fruits and vegetables, fat chickens and juicy steaks to the other passengers. Finally the aromas overpowered his fears, and he stopped a waiter.

"Please," he begged the surprised man. "I am weak from hunger. I'll do anything to earn a meal — clean rooms, swab decks, wash dishes . . ."

"Did you stow away?" the waiter asked. The man shook his head. "Then why haven't you eaten? The price of your ticket includes your meals. They're already paid for. You only have to come and eat!"

Do we live like spiritual stowaways when all the benefits of a first-class passage are ours to claim? How sad to condemn ourselves to cheese-and-cracker Christianity when Jesus invites us to "come and dine" with Him at the table of honor.

Is it possible that you believe in God and have given Him your life, yet you continue to live as though He does not exist? Do you ask Him to guide, then move on as if He does not care about your life? Are you ready to make a change and begin to draw on the incredible power of the Holy Spirit? He invites you to come to that turning point right now.

All it takes is faith: *trusting God to be just what He claims to be.* Jesus said we would be able to do even greater works than He did if we believe that He means what He says (John 14:12). Whatever we ask in His name, He says He will do (John 14:14). You do not have to live a defeated carnal, guilt-ridden life. You have a choice.

Our loving Lord commands us to come away from our carnality, and become the fruitful witnesses He calls us to be in John 15:16. The best part is that *He Himself has both the power and the desire to bring us to experiencing true love and forgiveness in Him.*

And so, as weak as our faith may be, we begin by placing it in a trustworthy God. That is the first step toward growth. Like a muscle, faith must be exercised if it is to become strong and useful.

We are like the man moving with great caution across a frozen lake in winter's cold. At first, he fears his next step will find him treading the black, freezing waters just below the surface. But every step that holds his weight confirms and increases his belief that the ice will hold his weight. When we place our trust in God the result will always be a stronger faith, for the better we know Him, the more we know he deserves our trust.

Other things — seemingly unimportant — have a surprising effect on our faith as it is maturing. I had a memorable demonstration of this one afternoon while playing with my small son. It was his turn to operate the controls of his model train set and for several minutes we enjoyed the wonderful little engine puffing around make-believe hills and valleys right on schedule. Then, for no apparent reason, it stopped. He tried the switch again but nothing happened. I took the little engine off the tracks and checked the connections; I wiggled the plug in the socket. Everything seemed to be as it should be, but the train would not go. Then my son spied a felled traffic sign at a crossing. Though not very big, it had fallen across the tracks, connecting the positive and negative rails and bringing the train to a stand still. The little sign had short-circuited the power.

Sin — even "unimportant" sin — can do the same thing in the life of a Christian. *It can never affect God's love for us.* That never changes! God loves us with an inexhaustible love. He loves us, not just "when" or "if" we deserve His love, but even when we are disobedient.

One of my most moving discoveries in my study of the Scriptures was the statement of our Lord in His high-priestly prayer to God the Father as recorded in John 17:23 (TLB): ". . . so that the world will know you sent me and will understand that you love them as much as you love me."

Think of it. God loves you and me as much as He loves the Lord Jesus Christ, His only begotten Son. Incredible! But true! Though God hates sin and will chasten or punish His children when we are disobedient, He never ceases to love us. "Whom the Lord loves, He disciplines " (Hebrews 12:6). In fact, He disciplines us because He loves us, not because He hates us. He hates only our sin.

And so if we want His uninterrupted power flowing through our lives, it is our responsibility to confess any known sin and experience afresh the wonder of God's forgiveness because of Jesus' death in our place. It is as necessary and natural to normal Christian life as breathing is to our physical existence.

In fact, it *is* breathing — spiritual breathing. We "exhale" by breathing out a confession to God, expelling the sin in our lives; we "inhale" as we breathe in the Holy Spirit, appropriating his fullness by faith. Spiritual breathing is a principle enabling us as believers to live consistent Christian lives. It is the "breath of life."

Consider with me the principles of spiritual "exhaling" as they apply to the Christian life. (We will discuss the process of spiritual "inhaling" in the following chapter.) We read in 1 John 1:9, "If we confess our sins, He [God] is faithful and righteous to forgive us our sins and to cleanse us from all unrighteousness." The word *confess* (in the Greek, *homologeo*) suggests agreement with God concerning our sins. Confession is a threefold process:

Acknowledgment of our sin. We need to be specific about our sin before God, and agree with

Him that what we have done is wrong, and grievous in His sight.

Acceptance of His forgiveness. We must also agree with God that Jesus' death on the cross bought the forgiveness we need for all our sins — past, present and future. We must accept the fact that there is nothing we can add to what He has done for us.

Repentance. We must repent, we must change our attitude toward sinning. The Holy Spirit offers us the power we need, and when we accept His power our conduct will change. Our sinful nature is no longer in charge. It is powerless under the control of the Holy Spirit. We are once again free to do what God wants us to do.

If you would like to breathe spiritually, there is a simple exercise you can do right now that will help you.

Humble yourself before God and ask the Holy Spirit to reveal to you sin that is in your life. With pencil and paper, list every sin that He brings to mind. Give Him sufficient time to show you the areas in your life which need change. Meditate on Psalm 32:1-6. Pray the psalmist's prayer in Psalm 139:23, "Search me, O God, and know my heart; test my thoughts. Point out anything you find in me that makes you sad" (TLB).

When you have completed your list, write across the top the indelible promise of 1 John 1:9:

IF WE CONFESS OUR SINS, HE IS FAITHFUL AND RIGHTEOUS TO FORGIVE US OUR SINS AND TO CLEANSE US FROM ALL UNRIGHT-EOUSNESS!

Now, destroy your list and thank God for His forgiveness and cleansing through His Son's death on the cross. His precious blood was spilled for *your sins.*

Keeping the channels open for God's power to flow through our lives lets us experience love and forgiveness in our Christian walk. It is the ingredient that transforms ordinary men and women into extraordinary, dynamic disciples of Jesus Christ!

RECOMMENDED ASSIGNMENTS

Chapter 2

Reflect: Several different descriptions of Christianity were presented in the opening pages of this chapter. Which illustration could I best relate to? Does my life lack power and peace?

Interpret: Read John 14 and 15. Reread the chapters, jotting down the incredible claims of Christ. Save this description of our trustworthy God for future personal reference.

Apply: Try a five-day experiment. Keep a personal journal of your spiritual journey as you begin practicing spiritual breathing. Record discoveries and victories.

CHAPTER THREE

HOW TO BE FILLED WITH THE SPIRIT

The first streams of morning light filtered through the small windows of the upper room and slipped across Peter's bearded face. He opened his eyes and raised up on one elbow. Most of the others were awake, rolling up their pallets and beginning the morning meal preparations for yet another day. *How much longer, Lord?* he wondered. For many days they had waited together in this small room, over a hundred of them now, just waiting for the Holy Spirit to come as Jesus had promised . . . .

And then he heard it. Like a strong windstorm in the distance at first, then the roaring sounds of violent, rushing winds right in the room. Louder and louder it sounded, and in their midst flaming tongues of fire resting on each one in the room, filling them with the Holy Spirit!

To say it changed their lives is an understatement! Suddenly these men and women of God were declaring the gospel of Jesus Christ with new confidence in a way that hearers understood, even to the point of preaching in languages they had never learned! They discovered an unquenchable power flowing from within them because they had been filled with the Source of Power Himself. And because of it, thousands followed them to a new and life-changing relationship with the risen Lord.

The book of Acts records for us the power of the Holy Spirit *at work in people's lives.* We read the stories and marvel at common people like you and me performing miracles and leading hundreds to Christ. Sadly we shake our heads, disappointed that we could not have lived then so we could have been a part of it all. We have all but conceded to the more "sophisticated" attitude that the Holy Spirit works among us only in subtle ways today. Peter and the others had to perform miracles to reach the lost with the gospel. Today many pass that idea off saying such "emotional displays" are no longer necessary.

But J. B. Phillips gives us insight on it when he writes in his introduction to *Letters to the Young Church:* "The great difference between present-day Christians and those of which we read in these letters [the New Testament epistles], is that to us it is primarily a performance; to them it was a real experience. We are apt to reduce the Christian religion to a code, or, at best, a rule of heart and life. To these men it is quite plainly the invasion of their lives by a new quality of life altogether. They do not hesitate to describe this as Christ living in them."

And if Christ still lives in His followers as He promised, should our lives be any less powerful than those of the disciples? For any Christian, life should be a great adventure. We have purpose, and we have the source of power needed to perform the tasks that fall to us. Jesus said, "He who believes in Me, the works that I do shall he do also; and greater works than these shall he do; because I go to the Father. And whatever you ask in My name, that will I do" (John 14:12,13).

But we are not expected to do these wonderful things in our own power. It is Christ Himself living within us who gives us the power through the Holy Spirit to do great works. All our wisdom and eloquence, logic, personality and good looks can never persuade someone to follow Christ, but with Jesus' resurrection power, His heart, His mind, His love for the lost flowing from within us, who could resist?

If we cannot see evidence of the power of the Holy Spirit in our lives, we need to take inventory and ask whether we are living as carnal Christians. If we are not, perhaps the reason for the absence of power is a lack of faith, or a lack of knowledge about who God and His Holy Spirit are.

Some years ago a West Texas rancher made a startling discovery.

The story goes that for Homer Yates, the end of the road seemed to have come too soon. As he rested a dusty boot on the running board of his weathered pick-up truck, he looked across acres of ranch land dotted with clusters of cattle. This valley was *his* valley. He and his family had called this land home for countless years.

This familiar scene had once brought peace to his heart. It had comforted him. But at this particular moment it triggered tears. He loved this place. How could he leave it behind? How could he be expected to pack up his belongings and walk away from the ranch he had poured himself into for so many years?

And yet what other choice was there now?

Things were all right until the depression hit. It came in like a swarm of devouring locusts and stripped him bare financially. He even had to accept government subsidy to keep the beloved ranch running marginally. It had shamed him to ask for help — but there seemed to be no other way. And as carefully as he and his wife had parceled out their meager funds, they never had quite enough. They had gone without, had sacrificed everything possible, but ruin was their reward.

Now, in the distance he saw another truck coming down the gravel lane carrying a couple of men, strangers to him. They rumbled to a stop a few yards away, dust settling around them in swirls as they closed in on him.

"Are you Yates?" one of them asked. He nodded. "We've been looking for you," he said, surprising Yates with a handshake. The tall one explained they were part of a geological crew sent by a major oil company, and they had reason to believe there might be oil on his land. Would he give them permission to drill a wildcat well on the other side of the ridge?

What could he lose? He signed the lease that afternoon. A little below eleven hundred feet they struck an oil reserve that was pumping 80,000 barrels a day before Yates knew what hit him. Several of the wells that followed yielded twice that amount. And Yates and his family owned it all!

Overnight, the humble rancher, scraping by on government relief, had become a multi-millionaire. He had lived in poverty on the very land that made him rich. The oil reserves had been there all along — all his since the day he signed the deed. But he *possessed it* only after he understood what riches were there, and that they were his for the taking.

How often we as Christians do the same thing, living like spiritual paupers when in truth, we are *children of the King*! Jesus described the Christian life as an exciting, abundant adventure, and for centuries many believers around the world have found it to be true.

Another problem we have is that we fear God will somehow take advantage of us if we give ourselves wholly to Him. We see in 1 John 4:18, "We need have no fear of someone who loves us perfectly; his perfect love for us eliminates all dread of what he might do to us. If we are afraid, it is for fear of what he might do to us, and shows that we are not fully convinced that he really loves us" (TLB). We can trust God with our lives once we begin to accept His love.

Imagine with me for a moment that you are the parent of a small boy whom you love keenly. One warm summer day he stands at your knees and struggles to tell you something of great importance to him. "I love you," he finally says, patting your hand, "and from now on I'm going to do everything you tell me to." You get down on one knee beside him, take his little shoulders in your hands and begin to shake him violently. You can see his eyes fill with terror as you shout, "I've just been waiting for this! Now I'm going to make things *miserable* for you. No more fun, no more toys, only hateful, horrible chores for as long as you live!"

What a strange response from a loving parent. We would expect to see tenderness and compassion shown toward the child, not a tirade like this. And yet, so often we fear the same kind of painful, punitive response from God if we should dare surrender ourselves to Him. A human parent would open their arms to their little one, welcoming them into an even deeper place of love. They would hope to merit such love from their child.

Why then do we expect anything less from God who loves us beyond human love? Is it that we do not understand His love for us? Matthew 7:11 describes God as a father demonstrative of his love for his children: "If you then being evil, know how to give good gifts to your children, how much more shall your Father who is in heaven give what is good to those who ask Him!"

Like Jesus who wept over Jerusalem, God looks at us and says, "How often I would have gathered you into My arms, but you would not let Me." If we are to be effective Christians we must begin — by faith — to trust the God of our salvation. From the time we accept His forgiveness to the time He walks with us through death, everything He gives us we receive by faith.

In chapter 2 we discussed the principle of "spiritual breathing," defining "exhaling" as the confession of sin and the acknowledgement of His love and forgiveness in our lives. Now we come to "inhaling."

Spiritual breathing would be as incomplete without the process of "inhaling" as would physical breathing. When obstructed breathing prevents oxygen from getting to the lungs, brains and vital organs, the human body dies. Proper spiritual breathing is of the same dramatic importance. To "inhale" spiritually is to draw deeply of the freshness of the Holy Spirit, appropriating by faith His fullness, giving Him free reign in our lives to control and empower us as He sees fit.

As we practice spiritual breathing, it becomes a natural habit. The constant, rhythmical "exhaling" (confession) and "inhaling" (appropriation of new power in our lives) creates a fresh, incomparable, daily approach to life.

But if we are to surrender our lives to Him, we must begin with an understanding of the nature and person of the Holy Spirit. You will notice I have not referred to Him as "it." The Holy Spirit is as much a person as God Himself. He is not some ethereal influence, or fleecy white spiritual concept. He is God. He possesses all the attributes that are ascribed to God the Father. As the third person of the trinity, the Holy Spirit is co-equal with God the Father and God the Son. There is only one God, but He manifests Himself in three persons.

Defining the trinity is a human impossibility. A seminary professor of mine used to say, "The person who denies the trinity will lose his soul. The person who tries to understand the trinity will lose his mind." Finite man cannot fully comprehend the infinite God.

It was the Holy Spirit who inspired men to write the Scriptures. As we read the Bible, He is the one who reveals its truth to us and helps us understand how to apply it to our lives. He makes our prayers heard by God, and it is He who reaps the harvest of our faithful witness. His sole purpose is to exalt and glorify Christ (John 16:1-15).

The evidence of the working of the Holy Spirit in the lives of believers is all around us. He has come to us, the Comforter that Jesus promised as He prepared to leave this earth. "It is to your advantage that I go away," Jesus said, "for if I do not go away, the Helper [Holy Spirit] shall not come to you; but if I go, I will send Him to you . . . . But when He, the Spirit of Truth, comes, He will guide you into all the truth . . . and He will disclose to you what is to come. He shall glorify Me; for He shall take of Mine, and shall disclose it to you" (John 16:7,13,14). Through new birth the Holy Spirit enables us to know Christ, and to share the Good News with others.

In 1 John 1:7 we are told, "If we walk in the light as He Himself is in the light, we have fellowship with one another, and the blood of Jesus His Son cleanses us from all sin." When we are filled with the Spirit, we are under His control; not as a robot, but as one led and empowered by the heart of God Himself. He walks this earth in our bodies, living His resurrection life in and through us.

Jesus said to the multitudes, "If any man is thirsty, let him come to Me and drink. He who believes in Me, as the Scripture said, *'From his innermost being shall flow rivers of living water'* " (John 7:37,38, italics ours). John adds, "But this He spoke of the Spirit, whom those who believed in Him were to receive" (John 7:39). We can live the victorious, power-filled lives that Jesus offers if we open our hearts to the indwelling presence of the Holy Spirit. The choice is ours.

But a question arises: *How?* How do we receive the Spirit into our lives? What do we do, what do we say so that He'll take up residence within us? So that we'll gain access to this marvelous power that is ours?

Suppose you have a bank account of several thousand dollars, and you need to cash a check. Would you walk into the bank, drop to your knees before a teller, and begin begging and pleading for the money you need? You smile because you know the surprised teller would probably lean over the counter and remind you, "You don't have to beg me. It's already your money. Just write out what you want and I'll cash your check."

The Holy Spirit is ours the day we accept Christ's forgiveness for sins. Like salvation, receiving the Holy Spirit is an act of faith. "For by grace you have been saved *through faith*" the Bible says, "and that not of yourselves, it is the gift of God; not as a result of works, that no one should boast" (Ephesians 2:8,9).

We need not beg or barter with God for His favor. Fasting, weeping, prostrating ourselves before Him will never cause Him to send His Spirit into our lives. We cannot *earn* God's fullness. It is only ours through *faith*, and it has been ours since the moment we became Christians. Colossians 2:6 reminds us, "As you therefore have received Christ Jesus the Lord, so walk in Him."

The Holy Spirit is ours. What we must learn to do now is *appropriate His power*. There are several factors that will help prepare our hearts as we seek to have lives filled with the Holy Spirit.

We must be hungry for the Spirit, and desire His indwelling. Jesus said, "Blessed are those who hunger and thirst after righteousness, for they shall be satisfied" (Matthew 5:6).

We must be willing to surrender our lives to Christ. In Romans 12:1,2 Paul writes, "I plead with you to give your bodies to God. Let them be a living sacrifice, holy — the kind he can accept. When you think of what he has done for you, is this too much to ask? Don't copy the behavior and customs of this world, but be a new and different person with a fresh newness in all you do and think. Then you will learn from your own experience how his ways will really satisfy you" (TLB).

Confess every sin. We need to let the Holy Spirit bring to mind everything that needs to be dealt with, then confess it all to God. We are promised in 1 John 1:9: "If we confess our sins to him, he can be depended on to forgive us and to cleanse us from every wrong. (And it is perfectly proper for God to do this for us because Christ died to wash away our sins)" (TLB).

With hearts opened and prepared for the filling of the Spirit, we are instructed in Ephesians 5:18 to "Be not drunk with wine, wherein is excess, but *be filled with the Spirit.*" It is a command! Not to be filled, controlled and empowered is disobedience. Scripture also tells us that there is available to us a "confidence which we have before Him, that, if we ask anything according to His will, He hears us. And if we know that He hears us in whatever we ask, we know that we have the requests which we have asked from Him" (1 John 5:14,15).

There is but one indwelling, one rebirth, and one baptism of the Holy Spirit — all of which occur at the moment of salvation. There are many *fillings*, made clear in Ephesians 5:18. In the original text, the meaning is more explicit than most English translations. This command means to be constantly and continually filled, controlled and empowered by the Holy Spirit *as a way of life!*

Technically, we do not even need to pray for the filling of the Holy Spirit as no Scripture tells us to do this. We are filled by faith. However, since the object of our faith is God and His Word, we can pray as an expression of our faith in God's command and in His promise. We are not filled because we pray but because we trust in God who responds to our faith.

Is this the desire of your heart? If you would like, pray this prayer:

"Dear Father, I acknowledge that I have been the one in control of my life, and as a result, I have disobeyed Your command to be controlled with the Spirit. Thank you for forgiving me, and now, Father, I invite Christ to take His rightful place on the throne of my life. In faith I ask You to fill me with Your Holy Spirit as You promised in Your Word. Thank You for keeping Your promises and for the indwelling of the Holy Spirit in my life right now."

If you prayed this prayer or expressed your heart similarly to God in your own words, you are now filled with the Holy Spirit. You do not have to "feel" like it; simply believe it as a fact — *in faith*. You can begin this very moment to draw upon the vast, inexhaustible resources of the Holy Spirit. He will enable you to live a holy life, to share the claims of Christ with seeking hearts in a new way.

Thank God for the fullness of His Spirit as you begin each day, and continue to invite Him to control your life, moment by moment. The Spirit-filled life is a life of supernatural power, of abiding in Christ, and of bearing spiritual fruit. It is trusting God, not self, to live the Christian life.

RECOMMENDED ASSIGNMENTS

Chapter 3

Reflect: Will the Holy Spirit *really* make a difference in my life? Will I still have problems? I'm going to find out this week. I'm going to allow the Holy Spirit to control and empower me. And because I am surrendering my will totally to Him, I believe I will . . .

Interpret: A supernatural life is the Christian's heritage. But theologians differ over the Holy Spirit's role in our lives. The fact is that Jesus Himself had much to say about the Holy Spirit (John

14:15-18; 15:26,27; 16:7-14; 20:21,22; Luke 11:13, etc).

Memorize the two key aspects related to being filled with the Holy Spirit: command (Ephesians 5:18), and promise (1 John 5:14,15).

Apply: Share this dynamic concept with a friend. Pray together that you will become obedient to the command to be filled. Pray that this discovery will give both of you supernatural responses to your current problems and concerns. Plan to get together in a week so you can share your victories.

CHAPTER FOUR

HOW TO
WALK IN THE SPIRIT

Chuck leaned on the horn one more time, a long, angry blast. He'd already been waiting ten minutes. Where were they?

Marianne knew how nervous he was about this morning, his first Sunday teaching the fifth grade boys. He had *asked* her and the kids to be ready *on time*! Finally she arrived, opened the door, and helped the three-year-old into the car.

"I can't believe this," Chuck shouted as six-year-old Julie cowered in the corner of the back seat. "I *told* you I had to be there early. I've got chairs to set up and materials to get ready!"

Marianne made a weak attempt to apologize as they pulled out of the driveway and headed — too fast — toward the church. Chuck ranted on with no consideration for his family's feelings . . . until something deep inside him seemed to say, "You're in a fine state of mind to be teaching about God's love and patience, aren't you?" He recognized the "voice" in an instant. It spoke quietly in the midst of his anger, and as always, dove right to the heart of the matter. He could not argue; he knew the voice was right.

He glanced at his wife. Just seconds before he had been so angry he had seen her as the enemy. Now what he saw was the woman he loved, staring sadly out the window as the houses slipped past beside them. He had wounded her deeply with his outburst.

"Honey," he said, reaching for her hand. "I owe you an apology." The rest of the trip they spoke quietly together, mending hurt feelings, righting wrongs, restoring their communication.

Chuck had slipped back into the practices of the carnal man like all of us at times. He had been so involved in the problem of the moment that he forgot who should be on the throne of his life. It is almost reflex to return to our carnal I'll-do-it-myself ways when we forget to believe the promises of God's Word (John 1:9), and their provisions for our daily living. We forget 1 Corinthians 10:13, "No temptation has overtaken you but such as is common to man; and God is faithful, who will not allow you to be tempted beyond what you are able, but with the temptation will provide the way of escape also, that you may be able to endure it."

Paul says in Romans 14:23, "Whatever is not from faith is sin." It is not sin itself that returns us to the carnal state again; it is what we decide to do about that sin. If we stop breathing spiritually and allow sin to separate us from God and/or our belief in His power for our lives, our only choice is to live once again as carnal Christians. On the other hand, as we choose to breathe spiritually — confessing our sins to God moment by moment (exhaling), and breathing deeply of His forgiveness and restoration (inhaling) — we continue to keep Him enthroned and to live victorious lives.

As Chuck drove his family to church that Sunday morning he "exhaled" when he confessed his sin to God and his family. And he "inhaled" a fresh filling of the Spirit as he opened his heart once again to God's restorative powers, and worked things through with his wife. When he stood before those fifth grade boys he was ready to speak to them with conviction of God's unconditional love for us as His redeemed children. The boys sensed in their teacher a humility and honesty that drew them to the Savior, and before class had finished three of the children had given their hearts to God. The Lord brings glory to Himself through the committed lives of His children.

As you "exhale" and "inhale" spiritually, you will notice a difference in your life. You will become "spiritually fit," and aware of a new freedom and power in your witness. When sin enters, do not let it set you back. Simply keep short accounts with God and do not allow sin to accumulate.

John writes, "My little children, I am telling you this so that you will stay away from sin. But *if you sin*, there is someone to plead for you before the Father. His name is Jesus Christ, the one who is all that is good and who pleases God completely" (1 John 2:1-6, TLB).

As your relationship with the Holy Spirit matures, you will discover it is both critical and progressive. It is critical, in that as you continue appropriating His power moment by moment, you will learn *how* to appropriate by faith what He offers you. Your relationship is progressive, in that, by faith, you will grow and mature in your Spirit-controlled walk. It is often easy to identify a believer who has walked in the Spirit for many years, for the fruit of the Spirit is easily seen.

The concept of "spiritual breathing" is a complex one, but it needs to be understood in a broader context. I would like to discuss four things we need to take precautions about in our Christian walk:

— being certain we are filled with the Holy Spirit;
— preparing for spiritual conflict;
— knowing our rights as children of God;
— living by faith.

In order to walk in the Spirit, we first must *be
sure that we are filled with the Spirit.* In Ephesians 5:18
we are told, "Be not drunk with wine, wherein is excess;
but be filled with the Spirit" (KJV). To be filled with
the Holy Spirit is to be controlled and empowered by
Him as a way of life. Jesus warned, "No one can serve
two masters; for either he will hate the one and love
the other, or he will hold to one and despise the other.
You cannot serve God and mammon" (Matthew 6:24).

There is a "throne" in each heart — our control
center — and there is room on the throne for only one
reigning power. The struggle within us is over control
of that throne, and the Christian who is ruled by self,
has removed the Holy Spirit from the throne of his life.

It is imperative that we remember God's *command*
to us, and His *promise.* He commands us, "Be filled";
He promises that if we ask anything according to God's
will, He will hear and answer (1 John 5:14,15). Because
He commands us to be filled with his Holy Spirit, we
can be sure that we are asking something that is in His
will for our lives. And when we pray according to His
will, He has promised to answer our requests. Therefore,
we can *expect* Him to fill and empower us when we
sincerely desire to surrender the control of our lives to
Him, and trust Him to fill us with His Spirit. Then we
must continue to breathe spiritually, "exhaling" by confession and "inhaling" by appropriating His forgiveness
and power in our lives by faith.

What about emotions in the experience of the
believer? Feelings add color and excitement, and are a
valuable part of life, but they are extremely fickle, changing with the weather. As Christians we live by *faith*,
trusting in God's trustworthiness and the promises of
His Word. If we depend on feelings for a confirmation
of His working in our lives, we put ourselves in a
dangerous position and will almost always be disappointed.

Let's compare the process of believing God and

living the Christian life to a train. The power is in the engine (FACT), the fuel is in the coal car (FAITH), and bringing up the rear is the caboose (FEELINGS). No engineer would couple his train to a caboose and expect it to pull the load. The engine — fact — gives Christianity its power, and often *feelings* follow naturally, as a bonus. But if they are not there it does not mean the *facts* have changed.

Refuse to seek emotional experiences as proof of the Holy Spirit's indwelling. If you have a sincere hunger and thirst for God's righteousness, and you have confessed your sin, surrendered to His control, and asked Him to fill you, you can be assured that *you are filled with the Holy Spirit!* God is faithful to His promises.

John 14:21 reminds us, "He who has My commandments and keeps them, he it is who loves Me; and he who loves Me shall be loved by My Father, and I will love him, and will disclose Myself to him." It does not say, "He who *feels love* for me," but, "He who *keeps My commandments.*"

Feelings usually follow the decisions and actions of our lives, but we need not look for them nor depend on them to confirm fact for us. Looking for an emotional experience is denial of the concept of faith, and whatever is not of faith is sin (Hebrews 11:6). When we believe God, He honors our faith and we can live life with assurance that He is filling us, moment by moment.

Second, as all good soldiers who are prepared for battle, we must be ready for spiritual conflict. We who have chosen to become spiritually alive and committed to our Lord, must *expect resistance from the enemy*, and one of his sharpest weapons is guilt. He will poke and prod when we least expect it, with stinging nettles that itch and swell. He will accuse us of sins for which we have already accepted God's forgiveness, and he will do everything possible to destroy our security in Christ, for he knows that a doubting soldier is worthless in battle. The good news is that we have a choice!

— Do not allow Satan to sink arrows into his target. A "moving target" is always harder to hit.

— Refuse to withdraw into *unnecessary introspection* (one of Satan's favorite ploys) and you will not probe into areas that have already been forgiven *and forgotten* by the Savior!

— Confess to God only what the Holy Spirit impresses upon your heart as something which is standing between you and His complete filling of your cleansed heart.

We are told in 1 Peter 5:7,8 to let God have all of our worries and cares, for He is always thinking about us and watching everything that concerns us. We are to be careful — alert to inevitable attacks from Satan, the great enemy, who prowls about the earth like a cunning lion looking for his next victim to tear apart. He is a shrewd and merciless foe, attacking either subtly or obviously, attempting to defeat and destroy us. But we can be confident that "greater is He who is in you than he who is in the world" (1 John 4:4).

Two thousand years ago Satan was defeated when Jesus Christ died on the cross for our sins. Victory is ours, *now*! We do not look forward to victory but backward, toward the cross where the enemy was defeated once and for all. We need not fear Satan as long as we walk in the Spirit, depending on Christ for our strength and provision.

The third area we must be aware of if we are to walk consistently in the Spirit is that of our rights as children of God (John 1:12). We have inherited an inexhaustible supply of love, power, forgiveness and grace from our Father. It is our responsibility to learn how to draw upon that supply.

The source book which declares our rights of inheritance is, of course, the Bible. As believers we need to spend time reading, studying, memorizing and meditating on God's Word to live in a way that will please Him.

The desires of His heart for us, His precious children, are hidden in the Scriptures. As we search for these nuggets of truth, they are revealed to us by the Holy Spirit Himself.

For example, when Christ takes up residence in our lives, our bodies become His living temples. Jesus promised us His special power to live holy lives (Romans 12:1,2). As His children, this is something we've inherited.

We also can be effective witnesses for Him. When His Spirit controls us, we are filled with His love for the lost, and as we share truth with them He speaks through us.

One word of caution. We must be careful not to think of Bible study, prayer and witnessing as "works" that justify our position in Christ. In truth, it is just the opposite. The works we do in the name of our Lord are the *results* of living to please the Savior, evidence of a lifetime given to the moment-by-moment filling of the Holy Spirit.

Finally, if we are to walk in the Spirit, we must live *by faith*. It is sad to see the pain of sincere Christians who have been deceived by a displaced emphasis on emotions. When unrealistic expectations are levied by others who have set their own standards of proof for the Spirit, there can be nothing but disappointment ahead. Praise God, we do not live by fluctuating feelings, but by faith in His never-changing Word!

And His Word is not silent on the issue of faith. Hebrews 11:6 tells us that "without faith it is *impossible* to please Him." Galatians 3:11 reminds us that we "live *by faith*."

Faith requires believing when it is not easy to do so. But God has given us a lifeline to hold fast to when things are rough. Romans 8:28 promises us, "all things . . . work together for good to those who love God, to those who are called according to His purpose."

It is not easy to learn to say, "Thank you, Lord,"

when your heart is breaking, but it is a priceless addition to the Christian walk. Writer Joseph Bayly, who has lost three sons in death over the years, has said that God was never closer than when he and his wife walked away from a fresh grave.

Praise and thanksgiving are gifts expressing our trust in God in the midst of overwhelming circumstances. Have you lost a loved one to death? Has pain and disease seemed to control your body? Have you received hurts you did not deserve? Have you suffered financial reverses? Have you tried thanking God, while none of it is making sense? Have you told Him you trust Him even when life is crushing in on you?

If we believe God and His promises when things seem to be falling apart around us, we are acknowledging His lordship, and obeying His command to trust Him when we cannot see the end. In 1 Thessalonians 5:18 we read: "In *everything* give thanks; for this is God's will for you in Christ Jesus." He promises rewards when we trust Him. He has said "all things" will work together for good, and He stands behind His Word.

It may seem that only a fool would be thankful under such circumstances but if we believe God's Word to be true, then we need to exercise our will and give thanks when there seems to be no reason for thanksgiving. Over the years Christians around the world have learned some sweet and valuable lessons through simply being *obedient* to God's Word, and giving thanks *when they least felt like it.*

To sum up, a Christian will want to walk in the Spirit moment-by-moment because God has commanded that we do so. It is the only way to keep Christ on the throne, and in control of our lives. And as self decreases and Christ increases (Galatians 2:20), the result will be unbelievable growth, and an abundant Christian life.

RECOMMENDED ASSIGNMENTS
Chapter 4

Reflect: The irritable, carnal Sunday school teacher in the first illustration of this chapter reminded me of somebody I know pretty well . . .myself! Why, just the other day, I . . . . It makes me stop and think. Whenever I catch myself experiencing downers like that, I can choose to confess my sins and become more spiritually fit. I really do want to begin walking in the Spirit, moment-by-moment.

Interpret: Examine Paul's letter to the Ephesians. The first chapter of this epistle focuses on our inheritance as believers. From that passage, make a list, with references from that chapter, entitled: "THANK YOU, LORD FOR . . . ."

Apply: Refuse to seek emotional experiences as proof of the Holy Spirit's indwelling. "Let heaven fill your thoughts" this week. Spend EXTRA time in the Word and allow the Lord to talk to you. Then you'll be prepared to go out your front door and tell others, whom the Holy Spirit has already prepared, about the peace and power you've found in Christ.

CHAPTER FIVE

HOW TO WITNESS IN THE SPIRIT

"It was awful," he said, shaking his head sadly. "I just froze. Right when I should have presented him with the gospel, I forgot everything I've ever heard about leading a friend to Christ. It was so awkward, so uncomfortable . . . for both of us." He stuffed his hands into the pockets of his jeans, "I guess I really blew it this time!"

No doubt my young frustrated friend is expressing some of the feelings we have all had when trying to lead someone to Christ. It is without a doubt the most important experience in a person's life, but when we are not prepared it can cause us much unnecessary confusion and discomfort.

The lost are hungry for Jesus Christ, but the majority of Christians have never led another soul to Christ, basically for two reasons: First, the average Christian does not live a victorious, Spirit-controlled life; and, second, most do not know how to communicate their faith in Christ to others effectively.

If you have been among the ranks of those who desire to share Christ but have not been as productive as you would like to be, the scriptural plan for witnessing on the next few pages will be of vital interest to you.

If taken to heart and practiced, it will give you the active, involved, and fruitful role you have hoped for in your everyday contact with people. It consists of eight simple steps, designed to help you become a fruitful witness.

1. Be certain you are a Christian.

There is no way a person who wants to introduce others to Christ can be used effectively unless he has first become a Christian himself. You must be sure that you have invited Jesus Christ to be the Lord and Savior of your life. It is the first and most indispensable step. It is where the Christian walk begins.

2. Confess any sin in your life.

We must be sure that there is no unconfessed sin in our lives, for sin separates us from God. We are sure to be "up-to-date" on this issue as long as we continue to breathe spiritually, "exhaling" to expel sin in regular confession to God.

3. Be filled with the Holy Spirit.

It is imperative that we be filled with the Holy Spirit, constantly "inhaling" spiritually to appropriate anew the limitless power He makes available to His children.

4. Be prepared to share your faith.

We must be prepared to share our faith in Christ with others whenever the occasion arises. Our seminaries and Bible schools are doing a wonderful job of preparing Christians to present the gospel of Jesus Christ in effective and dynamic ways around the world. Yet each of us can expect to be used of God right where we are, with nothing more than the knowledge we have gained today.

When we couple a willing heart with the empowering of the Holy Spirit, souls are won to Christ. A testimony that touches the hearts of the lost does not depend on professional training. The gospel of Jesus Christ is simple enough for any child to grasp, and we do not need degrees in theology to help people come to know Christ personally.

Jesus said, "All authority has been given to Me in heaven and on earth." And then He commanded us, "Go therefore and make disciples of all the nations, baptizing them in the name of the Father and the Son and the Holy Spirit, teaching them to observe all that I commanded you" (Matthew 28:18-20). But He never sends us out alone. The final words of Matthew's letter are a gentle promise to all Christians. Jesus said, "And lo, I am with you *always*, even to the end of the age."

Amazing as it seems, God has chosen to limit the expression of His love to human beings here on His earth. He has no arms but ours, no heart but ours, no voice without the voice of His children. We are a vital part of His plan to reach the rest of the world with His love. We are "carriers." Yet our only responsibility is to follow Him; it is up to Him to make us effective witnesses. If we are *obedient*, He will use us greatly in this exciting adventure to win the world!

5. Remember to pray.

We are to pray for those we hope to win to Christ. The Bible tells us that God is not willing that any should perish, but that all should come to repentance. "He isn't really being slow about his promised return, even though it sometimes seems that way. But he is waiting, for the good reason that he is not willing that any should perish, and he is giving more time for sinners to repent" (2 Peter 3:9, TLB). He also promises that if we ask anything according to His will, He will hear and answer. "And we are sure of this, that he will listen to us whenever we ask him for anything in line with his will. And if we really know he is listening when we talk to him and make our requests, then we can be sure that he will answer us" (1 John 5:14,15, TLB). The promise does not mean that everyone who hears the gospel will follow Christ, but there is no way we can tell who will choose Christ and who will reject Him. Though some will hear the gospel and choose to walk away, it is our responsibility — and privilege — to pray for the lost, for God honors our prayers.

Begin by making a prayer list and naming those whom the Holy Spirit lays on your heart. Then daily claim them for God; you have the authority to do this based on the Scriptures mentioned above. As you pray, continue to share Jesus' love in every way possible. We are not always able to *speak* the gospel; sometimes we are limited to *living* it quietly, but we can be confident that the seeds are being planted and the Spirit is at work! As the unsaved experience your unmerited love for them, the Holy Spirit will work in their hearts, drawing them to Himself in time.

Sometimes we are allowed to share in the joy of those we pray for as they turn their lives over to Christ. Others may require years to become Christians. Still others may appear "hopeless" in our eyes, refusing to accept any part of Christianity. Do not give up hope. God works in unpredictable ways. Just pray, and leave the outcome to the Lord.

6. Go tell others about Christ.

We do not have to wait for men to come to us. We can, and should, take the Good News to them. But one of the most difficult hurdles in witnessing is getting started. Satan loves to fill us with excuses: "I'm just too busy right now," or "I really don't know what to say to someone about Christ." We are not alone. The Holy Spirit goes with us. In fact, He has *preceded* us in every step, preparing the hearts of the people to whom we will speak. Jesus has told us to tell the Good News to all men. We can count on Him to uphold us and strengthen us as we do what He has asked us to do.

7. Talk about Christ.

Paul says, "Everywhere we go we talk about Christ

to all who will listen" (Colossians 1:28, TLB). Paul set a precedent for us to follow, but he was sensitive to his hearer's choice to listen. He did not force-feed the gospel. There will be some people who seem to insist on remaining on a superficial level with us, who refuse to open their ears or their hearts to the Good News. Though it may be frustrating, we must be sensitive to the leading of the Holy Spirit, in seeking *His timing*. He will lead, and make opportunities available as He sees fit.

When I was just a lad, my family used to visit my uncle's home in the country. For miles before we turned into the winding, gravel driveway to the big, old white house, I could smell the tantalizing perfume of fat, juicy peaches blowing through the open windows. Within minutes after our arrival, my Aunt Sara would send my cousin and me into the orchard to fill a bushel basket between us, and we would come back hours later, the basket and our bulging tummies full to overflowing.

It did not take me long to learn that the best peaches for picking — and eating — were the *ripe* ones! We left the green fruit on the trees until we were dispatched to the orchard again for another basketful. I soon discovered something wonderful had happened in our absence. The fruit that we had left on the trees because it was green and hard, had become pink-cheeked and juicy, just perfect for one of Aunt Sara's heavenly cobblers.

The same is true of witnessing. We must become sensitive to the "ripeness" of the heart receiving our witness. Some will be ready the first time they hear. Others will need time, and more prayer, before they will receive Christ into their lives. It is not our responsibility to pressure them into "making a decision for Christ." Consider leaving them with some well-chosen literature, and remain open to the leading of the Holy Spirit about talking to them further at a later time.

As those who are ready to consider the claims of

Christ become open to your witness, remember to
encourage them to invite Him into their lives. Many
hearts are ready to receive Him but are ignorant of
how to become a believer. Gentle, sensitive guidance,
often with an aid like the Four Spiritual Laws booklet,
will show them, step-by-step, how to turn their hearts
over to God's control. That aid also helps in keeping
the conversation centered on Christ without getting side-
tracked into distracting issues.

8. Expect hearts to respond to the gospel.

We can be confident in the power of the God of
creation. He is sovereign. He is omnipotent. And He is
not willing that any should perish. Like salespersons
who never get the hang of selling door-to-door, some
Christians approach the lost with a "you-wouldn't-be-in-
terested-in-becoming-a-Christian" attitude right off the
bat.

We have nothing to be ashamed of. The Lord of
our lives is the Lord of all, the King of kings! We need
to witness with a spirit of expectancy. God goes before
us to prepare hearts, to ripen them in His time. There
are those who wait without Christ, who are eager to
find Him.

Satan, the "father of lies," would have us believe
that people are not interested in finding God. We have
allowed ourselves to be deceived into thinking that
hearts will not be responsive to the gospel. But these
are crucial and exciting times in which we live today!
The Holy Spirit is at work among students, and lay
people, worldwide. People are coming to Christ in steady
streams. There is an insatiable thirst for Jesus Christ,
the living water (John 4:10-15).

Make no mistake, it is not religion that men and
women seek today. For the most part, they want nothing
to do with church and organized rules to live by. What
they do want is the experience of a real and vital
relationship with the Savior. Religion is man's search for
God. Christianity is so much more: It is God's revelation

of Himself to man in the person of Jesus Christ. If, in love, we confront people with the claims of Christ, we will see many respond to His love and forgiveness. But the responsibility for their decision rests with the Holy Spirit.

We at Campus Crusade for Christ sincerely believe that success in witnessing is simply sharing Christ in the power of the Holy Spirit and *leaving the results to God.*

Learn these easy-to-follow guidelines for witnessing in the Spirit. Put them to work in your life and watch the results. If you have been sitting on the witnessing sidelines watching others win people to Christ, this will change your life . . . and the lives of those who hear the gospel because of you!

RECOMMENDED ASSIGNMENTS

Chapter 5

Reflect: Just wondering. . . . When I think of the word "witness", how many different meanings come to mind? Is it *enough* to be a "silent witness" by my actions? Have I already become a fruitful witness for Christ, or am I still in the process?

Interpret: In Colossians 1:28, Paul writes, "Everywhere we go we talk about Christ to all who will listen" (TLB). Where in the world *did* Paul go? The apostle set a precedent for us to follow. With a Bible dictionary in one hand, and a map of Paul's missionary journeys in the other, research specific examples of WHERE and HOW Paul spread the gospel in his first-century world.

Apply: This week, thank the Lord that the Holy Spirit enables you to be an effective witness for Him. Look for an opportunity at work, in

your neighborhood or at the mall to spontane-
ously tell someone about the difference that
Jesus Christ makes in your everyday world.

CHAPTER SIX

HOW TO INTRODUCE OTHERS TO CHRIST

"I can't get over the change in my husband since he's begun sharing the gospel with others," Margaret said. "He shows the Four Spiritual Laws booklet to everybody — students, fellow teachers, policemen, garage mechanics." She laughed, "You should have seen him sharing it in the pool with water up to his neck! And you know what the best part is? He doesn't stop. People just keep coming to Jesus."

Of all life's experiences, sharing Christ is the most rewarding because of what it means to each person's eternal state. Once we discover Christ for ourselves and grow to love Him, it is only natural to want others to know Him as we do. But there are other reasons for sharing the gospel, too. We want to look at seven of them. (Later in this chapter, we will discuss some practical "how-to's" for introducing people to Christ.)

1. We are constrained by love.

Paul writes "For the love of Christ controls us, having concluded this, that one died for all, therefore all died; and He died for all, that they who live should no longer live for themselves, but for Him who died and rose again on their behalf" (2 Corinthians 5:14,15). Because we have experienced God's love and forgiveness in our own lives, we want everyone around us to experience this same love.

2. We are commanded by Christ.

Christ commanded us to be witnesses for Him. He said, "Follow me." The purpose? "I will make you fishers of men" (Matthew 4:19). In John's Gospel Jesus said again, "You did not choose Me, but I chose you, and appointed you." Why? "That you should go and bear fruit" (John 15:16).

3. Men are lost.

Those without Christ are lost, separated from God eternally unless they are shown the way to God. So we want to try to introduce everybody we meet to Christ. Jesus claims, "I am the way, and the truth, and the life; no one comes to the Father, but through Me" (John 14:6). God's Word emphatically declares, "There is salvation in *no one else*! Under all heaven there is *no other name for men to call upon to save them*" (Acts 4:12, TLB).

4. Benefits are received.

We want to share our faith in Christ because of the benefits to those who receive Him. John 1:12 tells us that when we introduce someone to Him, that person becomes God's child. His body becomes the temple of the living God (2 Corinthians 6:16), and his sins — past, present and future — are forgiven (Colossians 1:14). The new believer experiences the peace of God (John 14:27), receives God's direction and purpose for his life (Psalm 37:23), and experiences the power of God to change his life (2 Corinthians 5:17).

5. We will experience spiritual growth.

We want to witness because we'll benefit from following God's command to share our faith. Witnessing leads us to grow stronger in our prayer life, and in our ability to study God's Word. It forces us to depend upon Christ and not self, for strength and direction. As we witness in the power of the Holy Spirit, we sow love, joy and peace in the lives of those around us.

According to Galatians 6:7, we will reap in our own lives exactly what we sow in the lives of others, and many times more than what we have sown. It behooves us to sow the fruit of the Spirit and avoid sowing vengeance and wrath.

6. It is a tremendous privilege.

Personal evangelism is an unparalleled privilege given to the children of God. In his second letter to the Corinthians, Paul wrote, "We are Christ's ambassadors. God is using us to speak to you: we beg you, as though Christ himself were here pleading with you, receive the love He offers you — be reconciled to God" (2 Corinthians 5:20, TLB).

It is a high honor to serve as an ambassador. As believers in Christ, we are ambassadors for the King of kings and Lord of lords!

7. We receive the power to witness.

We can practice way-of-life evangelism because the Holy Spirit empowers us to witness. Jesus Christ said, "You shall receive power when the Holy Spirit has come upon you; and you shall be My witnesses" (Acts 1:8). To fail to witness for Christ is to deny the Holy Spirit His right to empower and to use us to introduce others to God's Son.

Let's remind ourselves again and again that training, materials, methods, techniques and strategies are of no value apart from the enabling, empowering Holy Spirit.

The story goes that Fred Brown cut himself doing chores one day and had to make a visit to old Doc Parker for some stitches. The country doctor sewed his neighbor up, good as new.

"That'll be fifty bucks, Fred," he said.

"Fifty bucks?" the patient echoed. "For six stitches?"

"I'm only charging five for the stitches," the wise old doctor replied. "The rest is for the know-how."

In introducing others to Christ it is "know-how" that will make the difference between an effective and an ineffective presentation. We witness in two ways: by the way we live, and by the words we speak. We are commanded to speak the Good News. This is the aspect of witnessing we will discuss in the remaining part of this chapter.

The town skeptic had come for dinner. He was a grandfatherly old man, good to the children and liked by the townspeople, but all his life he had looked down his nose at religion, and seemed to think Christians paddled their boats without oars. But the couple whose table he sat at now loved the Lord, and had recently seen their teenage son, Mark, give his heart to the Savior.

After dinner Mark and the old man had been alone in the parlor for just a few minutes when the boy slipped a small booklet from his wallet and handed it to the skeptic. "See what you think of this," he said.

The older man squinted at the print and slowly worked his way through the few tiny pages. As he reached the prayer at the end, he looked up with tears brimming in his eyes. "Is this what you and the other Christians have been trying to tell me all these years?" Mark nodded. "Well, why didn't you *say so*?" And the skeptic gave his heart to God.

In presenting the gospel to non-Christians you'll want a simple approach. The tool we have seen used most effectively at Campus Crusade for Christ is, of course, the Four Spiritual Laws booklet. It contains all the essential truths an unbeliever needs in order to recognize his need for Christ. It helps a person make a decision to ask Christ into his heart.

We do not claim that this particular presentation

is the only way to introduce others to Christ, or even the best way, but we have seen tens of thousands of people receive Christ through its direct, simple presentation of the gospel. Millions of copies of this unassuming booklet have been distributed in major foreign languages. Several wordless versions, illustrated for remote cultures, have been released recently.

Many are skeptical about using the Four Laws. Some feel that anything so condensed must be incomplete. One typical objector was an assistant pastor at a large metropolitan church. He was given a booklet but, prejudiced by bad experiences with tracts, he refused to read it, tossing it carelessly on his desk.

Several days later a city inspector came to the church to inspect the facilities. As the woman was about to leave, it suddenly occurred to the young minister that he was about to miss an opportunity to share Christ. Quickly he looked around for something to give her, to take with her as she left. There lay the Four Spiritual Laws booklet he had tossed aside.

"Here," he said, handing her the booklet. "Read this."

Thinking that he meant "read it now," the woman began to read the booklet aloud, every word, page by page. Midway through the simple message, tears began slipping down her cheeks. Standing beside an amazed minister she led herself to Christ.

The results are fruitful because the message is clear. It is empowered by the Holy Spirit who goes before us, preparing hearts.

A tool such as the Four Spiritual Laws booklet enables us to:

> open the conversation easily;
> begin with a positive statement;
> present the gospel clearly and simply;
> be confident in our witnessing because we know what we are going to say and how it should be said;

be prepared and able to stick to the subject without getting off on tangents;
be brief, thorough, and to the point;
offer suggestions for growth in the new Christian;
learn a "transferable technique" that can be passed on to the new believer, who can be encouraged to lead others to the Savior.

Many who are effective in their own personal ministries are unable to communicate this skill to their children so that they can communicate the plan of salvation to *their* spiritual children, generation after generation. But this is the very thing Paul exhorted Timothy, his young son in the faith, to do.

"For you must teach others those things you and many others have heard me speak about. Teach these great truths to trustworthy men who will, in turn, pass them on to others" (2 Timothy 2:2, TLB).

Using the Four Spiritual Laws, even the brand new Christian can show friends and loved ones how they, too, can find freedom in Christ.

If someone were to ask what you thought was the hardest part of witnessing, what would you answer? Many who come to Campus Crusade headquarters for evangelism training have said that for them the most difficult part of sharing the gospel was *getting started!* Even those of us who have shared Christ often enough to be called "seasoned" occasionally experience attacks of insecurity when we are witnessing.

Some time ago I was in Dallas, Texas, sharing with a group of pastors and chaplains. A university chaplain in the group asked if I would go with him to a nearby campus to demonstrate how to use the Four Spiritual Laws booklet in witnessing to students. I agreed, and after we arrived on campus, he gathered a dozen or so young people around so I could share.

Even as I handed out the booklets to these bright young people, I was beginning to receive negative impressions within me from the enemy. "These students are bright. They're going to laugh you right off campus with this simple little booklet. You need something more sophisticated, better geared to their needs. . . ."

But I proceeded, silently reminding Satan that I was free from his power because Jesus said, "Greater is He who is in you than he who is in the world" (1 John 4:4). I asked everyone to read silently while I read the booklet aloud just as I had done thousands of times before.

The feeling of uneasiness did not leave, but I continued reading until we came to the prayer. Suddenly I was bombarded with what seemed like a chorus of voices warning me that if I prayed that prayer I would be labeled a fool by these young people. But I read the prayer without taking a breath, and said to the little group surrounding me, "If this prayer expresses the desire of your heart, pray it with me silently as I read it again. Make it your own prayer."

When I looked up there were tears running down the cheeks of one young woman. She said that she had prayed the prayer and knew that Jesus Christ had come to live in her heart. Just as we were leaving the campus a young man from the group found us and asked us to help him receive Christ. As we pulled away from the school, the chaplain told me of a third young person who also had received Christ.

I had struggled internally regarding both my acceptability and the credibility of the material I was sharing with these students. But I shared the gospel message out of obedience, not because I felt like doing it, and the Spirit of God was at work in the students' hearts, making them aware of their need for Him, and showing them the way of salvation.

We discussed in depth, in earlier sections of this book, how important it is for us not to live by our feelings. We operate from fact, and the fact is that it is Christ Himself who wins souls — not us. The opportunity to share arises in myriad ways. We simply need to begin. We start by trusting God for His promised strength and sensitivity as we share our faith in obedience to His command.

Ours is a self-centered culture. It's a struggle to develop sensitivity to the needs of others. The next time you are at a lecture, a class, or a gathering of some kind, introduce yourself to someone. Initiate conversations whenever you are standing around on a break, or milling about after a meeting.

At a social event, you might begin a conversation by asking someone what they thought of the program. As you begin talking, be alert to opportunities that might turn the conversation toward the Lord. Do not try to make it happen. Maintain a natural progression of conversation, but grab a chance when further questions could lead the discussion toward God. As you prayerfully depend on the Holy Spirit for guidance, He will give you wisdom in making transitions flow naturally.

Be alert for a creative opportunity to show someone the Four Spiritual Laws booklet. Ask that person to read it with you. If he or she has already heard of the Four Laws, ask "What is your opinion of it?" Review the booklet with the person and give him or her an opportunity to receive Christ at this time.

Keep in mind that although millions have been prepared to receive the gospel and make a decision for Christ, you will encounter some whose hearts are not prepared. Be careful not to offend the one with whom you are sharing Christ. Never badger or manipulate. Don't press for a decision. Jesus reminds us, "No one can come to Me, *unless the Father who sent Me draws him*" (John 6:44).

What counts is not what you do, but what the Holy Spirit does through you (1 Corinthians 3:6). You and I have neither the ability nor the responsibility to bring anyone to Christ. Remember: *Success in witnessing*

*is simply sharing Christ in the power of the Holy Spirit
and leaving the results to God.*

If someone is *not* ready to accept Christ, you'll
want to leave this individual with a positive impression
of true Christianity. Maintain a positive and loving attitude
toward him, regardless of his decision. Give him the
booklet. Try saying something like, "You may want to
receive Christ one day. Let me show you what will
happen when you do invite Him into your life."

If he is receptive, go on to explain assurance of
salvation by reading the rest of the booklet with him.
If his response is positive, consider giving him another
chance at that point to pray with you to receive Christ.

If the person you have shared the plan of salvation
with prays the prayer, your next aim is to lead him
through the steps to assurance of his salvation. The
material in the booklet which follows the prayer is
designed to help the new Christian be sure of his
salvation.

Ask the new Christian whether he received Christ
into his life, and where he believes Him to be right
now. If his reply is somthing like, "Well, He's in the
world," or "He's in heaven," show him Revelation 3:20.
Explain that we can *know* Christ is in our hearts based
on the authority of God Himself and His Word. Read
1 John 5:11-13 with the person, emphasizing that we
can know we have eternal life on the basis of these
promises from God's inspired Word.

Follow-up is of vital importance. It cannot be overemphasized. Try to secure the name and address of
each individual with whom you pray. Then, whenever
possible, arrange to meet together for spiritual counsel
and follow-up within the next two days.

Whether you are able to meet with the new Christian or not, send his name and address to Campus
Crusade for Christ, Arrowhead Springs, San Bernardino,
CA 92414. He will immediately be added to our follow-
up list and be sent a series of Bible study letters. He

also will receive materials emphasizing assurance of salvation, how to read the Bible, how to pray, the ministry of the Holy Spirit in our lives, baptism, service, and sharing Christ with others.

One young woman said, "After I became a Christian I was just plagued with doubts about my salvation, and then I began receiving letters from Campus Crusade. At first I resented them and whoever was sending them to me. Then slowly, I began to read the letters, and the answers I needed so desperately to know were there! I finally surrendered my will to Christ and have just been accepted onto the staff of Campus Crusade! Without that follow-up, I wouldn't be serving God today."

RECOMMENDED ASSIGNMENTS

Chapter 6

Reflect: When I prayed to invite Christ into my life, how much of the gospel did I know? Did I have an in-depth grasp of the doctrine of salvation? Did I understand theology? NO! As I best recall, I simply. . . .

Interpret: "Words and Their Meanings" is not just an exercise for English teachers and writers! Believers who want to grow in their faith in Christ know that they need to spend quality time in God's Word. And that kind of study involves digging into the meaning of topics, phrases, and words. Here's an idea. Use a Bible with cross references to look up each of the verses mentioned in the Four Spiritual Laws. Ask God to give you fresh insights into familiar words. Think of unbelievers hearing these words for the first time. Make note of your current discoveries.

Apply: Try these tips to enhance your witnessing presentation. Secure a copy of the Four Spiritual Laws booklet. With a highlighter pen, mark the phrases you want to be sure to emphasize every time you share your faith with others. With a red ink pen, insert this remark across the top of the first page: "That's a good question. Let's talk about it after we have completed the booklet." (Try to remember this response when "smoke-screen" questions arise.) Go through each page of the booklet, jotting down a few remarks and/or illustrations you may want to use to personalize each presentation.

CHAPTER SEVEN

HOW TO
HELP FULFILL
THE GREAT COMMISSION

Today we would call it a strategy meeting; the "Coach" and the "players" together in a "huddle" on a mountain in Galilee. The risen Lord had a plan, one that would reach the entire world. Christians call this global strategy "the Great Commission." What was said on the mountain has affected generation upon generation of believers. Had it not, few today would be experiencing the love and forgiveness of God's grace.

The disciples leaned close as Jesus said, "All authority has been given to Me in heaven and on earth. Go therefore and make disciples of all the nations, baptizing them in the name of the Father and the Son and the Holy Spirit, teaching them to observe all that I commanded you" (Matthew 28:18-20). It was the greatest promise ever recorded!

In this chapter we will be looking at the who, what, why, when, where and how of the Great Commission.

Who mobilized the Great Commission? And to whom was it directed?

Who would dare claim "all authority . . . in heaven and on earth"? There could be only one answer. It would have to be the unique God/Man Himself, Jesus Christ, the very Son of God. At Jesus' birth, God became man. He allowed other men to put Him to death on a cross, but three days later was raised from the dead. His death and resurrection saved the human race from the power of sin and provided eternal life for all who would believe. The result was a spiritual revolution that upset the first century world and altered the course of history.

As Christ walked the earth He had the power to change lives. That same life-changing power is available today. His life spans centuries because He was — and is — God! Though it was His disciples who heard Him speak the words of the Great Commission, their impact continues to apply to all Christians throughout history.

It is a supernatural plan given by the infinite God to finite man. So often we slip into thinking that the early Christians were different from us — that they possessed a quality of life we cannot attain. But the men and women who heard Jesus' words were common, ordinary, working people, plagued with the same weaknesses that we are. Two outstanding things happened to them.

First, they knew a resurrected Lord, triumphant over death, one who lived among them and promised He would return to reign as King over all the earth.

Second, they were filled with the Holy Spirit.

We have the same opportunities to be committed to our resurrected and returning Lord. His Holy Spirit waits to empower those of us who ask for His filling. We have the *same ability to turn our world upside down*! We could start a revolution in the 20th century that would rival anything the world has seen thus far!

What is the Great Commission?

The command of our Lord simply means winning hearts to Jesus, teaching them what He taught, equipping them to send them out as ambassadors in such numbers that every soul in the world would hear the message heralded by angels the night our Lord was born: "I bring you the most joyful news ever announced, and it is for *everyone*! The Savior — yes, the Messiah, the Lord — has been born tonight in Bethlehem!" (Luke 2:10,11, TLB).

But, wait a minute, you say. This old world has almost four billion people in it. Surely you can't be serious about telling *everyone* about Christ? Oh yes we can!

To those who laugh at the possibility of achieving a task of such magnitude we point to benefits surrounding those of us living in this exciting century. Consider for a moment the giant strides technology has made even in our generation. The media has brought the edges of our task to within our grasp. Let me give you an example.

A man by the name of John Heyman produced a film, simply entitled *Jesus*. In the years since its release, its evangelistic impact around the world has been staggering. A copy of the picture can be dubbed perfectly into *any language* within a matter of weeks using generators, jungle recording studios, and native voice actors.

The dubbed film lessened the need for a linguist to learn a tribal tongue, reduce it to written symbols, translate Scripture and teach a people to read so that the gospel can be shared. This is an enormous task and takes years to accomplish. The film has made it possible for tens of thousands of people around the world to have committed their lives already to the Jesus they have learned about. *Jesus* gives them the message of salvation *in their own tongue*. Skeptics, we are on our way!

**Why should Christians devote themselves com-
pletely to fulfilling the Great Commission?**

There are at least three good reasons:

1. *We obey because Christ commanded us to go.*
The athletic coach presents his list of rules and standards
to his players and says, "These are the things you must
do if you expect to be on the team." Players abide by
the rules, or they don't make the team. In battle, the
commanding officer shouts orders to his soldiers who
obey without question or face the threat of court-martial,
or even death. Jesus' authority is based on love, and
backed by God the Father, and He has issued us an
order: "Go!" We dare not take our Lord's command
lightly.

2. *We obey because men are LOST without Christ.*
Jesus said, "I am the way, and the truth, and the life;
no one comes to the Father, but through Me" (John
14:6). That may sound narrow, but God Himself has
said it. I dare not choose to argue with my Lord.

3. *We obey because hearts are hungry for God.*
Since the beginning of the ministry of Campus Crusade
for Christ, we have witnessed man's hunger for God
demonstrated in thousands of ways. As part of our
worldwide training program, trainees spend hours each
week in person-to-person evangelism in local communities, on beaches and in public gatherings. It is not
unusual for hundreds in a single afternoon to pray to
receive Christ.

Just recently, more than *three thousand* Blacks in
south-central Los Angeles received Christ through the
personal contact of some sixteen hundred staff and
student workers. *Over two thousand* asked Christ into
their lives in one day of sharing on the beaches of
Southern California.

In similar situations nine thousand Korean trainees
shared Christ with some *forty-two thousand people* in
a single afternoon of witnessing. *Sixteen thousand ex-*

pressed a desire to receive Christ, and *four thousand* appropriated the power of the Holy Spirit by faith.

When will the Great Commission be fulfilled?

Only Jesus and His Father know when and how it will be done. However, since He gave us the command, and has promised to equip us to do His will, we must assume that He means for us to pursue the fulfillment of His design in each generation . . . an *on-going process* of fulfilling the Great Commission.

If it is to be fulfilled at all, *now is the time for action*. We must begin now, and dedicate ourselves daily — as a way of life — to communicating God's love and forgiveness to those our lives touch. As the apostle Paul writes in Colossians 1:28, "So *everywhere we go we talk about Christ to all who will listen*" (TLB). From the time we awaken in the morning until we go to bed at night, our first priority is sharing the most joyful news ever announced to hearts aching to hear it.

Where do we fulfill the Great Commission?

We must reach the whole world — a discouraging impossibility for mere human beings. But Jesus laid down a strategy to follow. Just before He ascended into heaven, Jesus told the disciples, "You shall be My witnesses both in Jerusalem and in all Judea and Samaria, and even to the remotest part of the earth" (Acts 1:8).

Jerusalem was home to the disciples with surrounding Judea also being familiar territory. But Samaria was the land of Gentiles, foreigners who knew nothing of Jewish beliefs, and it was the edge of the "uttermost part of the world."

Where does "Jerusalem" begin for us? Where all journeys begin, at home. Our home lives can reflect the love that Jesus channels through us. From there that love will overflow into our neighborhoods, our campuses and classrooms, our jobs and all our involvements. The next logical step will be on to "Judea," our communities and states, our nations. And from there it is a small step beyond into "Samaria and the uttermost part of the world" The Great Commission is immobile unless we see our part and become personally involved in our homes and communities, and eventually our world!

Oh, what an exciting hour for Christians to get involved. We are on the brink of the greatest spiritual awakening since Pentecost! What men see as a dark and desperate hour is truly an hour of destiny for Christians, the hour for which we were born. It is time to shine like beacon lights and set in motion a sweeping spiritual revolution that will reveal to mankind the glorious gospel of Christ, the answer to every question.

Don't get caught on the sidelines. Get involved! Do *your part* to help fulfill the Great Commission in *this generation!*

How do we share what we have?

Men everywhere are lost and we who belong to Christ have the answer. When He said, "Go!" Jesus made it clear that this "answer" is to be shared. It is His will that we be actively involved in helping to fulfill His command — His Great Commission. And yet the questions linger: What does God want *me* to do? How do I begin?

We begin by developing individual, personal strategies that tie directly into the global strategy of our Lord. It is the only way this great task will be accomplished.

And what is a personal strategy? It is an individual's deliberate plan of action to accomplish a specific goal. Since our goal is to help fulfill Christ's command, our personal plans should include evangelizing and discipling — adding to the Body of Jesus Christ, and multiplying believers.

Spiritual addition is simple: One believer + the gospel + one non-believer = two believers. Spiritual multiplication is a little different. The formula is: One believer + one new believer + discipling = two believers evangelizing and discipling others. Spiritual multiplication is deliberately discipling new Christians *so that they will evangelize and disciple still others.*

Paul specifically commended this principle to Timothy, his "son" in the faith, when he said "The things which you have heard from me in the presence of many witnesses, these *entrust to faithful men, who will be able to teach others also*" (2 Timothy 2:2).

A personal strategy enables us to move forward in obedience to help fulfill the Great Commission. Paul said, "No soldier in active service entangles himself in the affairs of everyday life, so that he may please the one who enlisted him as a soldier" (2 Timothy 2:4).

"All right," you say, "I'm convinced. I need to have a personal strategy. But where do I begin to develop a plan that will work in my life?" Allow me to make some simple suggestions based on Scripture.

Be committed to Christ and filled with the Holy Spirit. Of the millions of people active in churches, a frightening percentage are either not certain they are born again, or are living frustrated, carnal lives, so far off-course that they cannot be used of God until they commit their lives to Him. If you struggle with a lack of faith, deal with it. Learn how to trust God, and He will take it from there.

Pray in faith that God will guide you in developing your personal strategy. Ask Him to reveal an effective plan to you to reach your immediate area of influence with the gospel. He already has one designed; your part is discovery, and that usually happens a little at a time.

Jesus' life was a perfect example of discovering the Father's plan. He presented every major decision to God, and waited for divine direction at each turning point. As you pray, *expect God to provide* the strategy, the wisdom, and the strength to implement it. Expectant faith pleases God.

Outline the plan God reveals in answer to your prayers. List the names of specific people and groups in your life, and develop a plan to reach each one. Begin with your family. Your home, more than any other place, will reflect your testimony. Trust God continually to fill you with His Spirit so that your actions bear witness to what He has done in you.

Plan to reach the people at work. Seek out those who you know are Christians, and ask them to join you in evangelizing your office or plant. In your church, make yourself available to teach Sunday school, and to be a part of (or begin) visitation evangelism teams. Be an encouragement to other members of your church.

Invite neighbors in for coffee or dessert with an evangelistic emphasis. Start a neighborhood Bible study with an evangelistic bent. Tell others what Christ has done in your life, and that He can do the same in theirs.

Learn everything you can that will help accomplish your personal strategy. Thousands of students, laymen and pastors take advantage of the training and materials available through Campus Crusade for Christ every year. They learn effective skills for winning men and women to Christ, building them in the faith, and sending them to the work with the good news of God's love and forgiveness. Leadership Training Institutes for college and high school students, and Lay and Pastors' Institutes for Evangelism offer both basic and advanced courses the year round.

Don't wait. Write out your personal strategy today. List the names of people God has placed on your mind and heart. Share Christ with them and add to the body of believers. Ask God for specific names of those He would like you to train to multiply spiritually with you.

Practice aggressive evangelism! *Take the initiative in fulfilling your part of the Great Commission* right where you live. Claim your relatives, friends, neighbors, and business associates for Christ in prayer. Then present the gospel to them. Tell them of the love and forgiveness Jesus waits to give them and allow them an opportunity to receive Him.

Share your faith as a way of life. It will become natural to talk about Christ with everyone you meet. As the people on your list begin to trust Him as Lord and Savior, disciple them and involve them in the cycle of spiritual multiplication. Encourage them to join you in an effort to saturate your entire area with the message of Jesus Christ.

As you implement your personal strategy locally, ask God's guidance to stretch your thinking beyond local goals to worldwide responsibilities. Discover ways you can become a world-conscious Christian and make a contribution to help spread the gospel overseas. Inquire about the missions program in your own church.

In these days of change and chaos, sincere, thinking Christians dare not be satisfied with the status quo, or business as usual. Whoever and wherever you are, when you make yourself available to God, expect to be used to help change the world! Changed hearts make a changed world. Jesus specializes in changing lives, but He can only reach men and women through us. Let Him start with you!

If your desire is to help fulfill the Great Commission make the following your prayer:

"Dear Father, I am available to You to do with as You wish. Work through me to bring Your message of love and forgiveness to hearts that hunger to hear. Cleanse me, empower me, use me to bring honor and glory to Your name. Enable me by Your Holy Spirit to give my best to help fulfill Your Great Commission in my time. In the sweet name of Jesus I ask this. Amen."

If you prayed this prayer, I wish you Godspeed in your endeavors. Prepare yourself for a great adventure. Investing your time, your talent and your treasure, you will be fulfilling the Great Commission of Christ in this generation. Your commitment is to Jesus Christ, not Campus Crusade for Christ, but if we can help in any way, we are available to serve you. Through the power of the indwelling Christ *you* can help change the world!

RECOMMENDED ASSIGNMENTS

Chapter 7

Reflect: The disciples were fortunate. They not only got to spend lots of personal time with Jesus — but they also were there with Him on the mountain when He revealed His plan for spreading the gospel. He taught it . . . and they caught it. That was *thousands* of years ago, yet someone came and told *me* that same Good News. . . .

Interpret: Every believer is both a "goer" and a "sender" in the task of fulfilling the Great Commission. Explore the scope and global strategy described in these passages: Matthew 28:16-20; Acts 1:8; Matthew 10; Luke 9:57-62; John 15:16-27; Acts 28:23-31.

Apply: What kind of an investment are you going to make toward the fulfillment of the Great Commission? Get started today. Carefully, prayerfully, write out your personal evangelism and discipleship strategy. Refer to the guidelines in this chapter. Follow Acts 1:8 for an "outline" of your goals. But don't just scribble it down on a scrap piece of paper — put it in a place where you'll see it often (i.e., on the fly-leaf of your Bible, in your prayer notebook, in your journal, on your yearly goal chart, on a 3" x 5" card over the kitchen sink, etc.). Be creative!

CHAPTER EIGHT

HOW TO
LOVE BY FAITH

Maybe you've known someone like Georgia . . . you wouldn't class her as a friend, but she's not an enemy either. She's a person you tolerate because she shares an office in the same suite as you. She says she attends church, but she doesn't act like a child of God. Her conversation is sprinkled with four-letter words and laced with the most recent "news" about fellow employees.

You have kept your distance because you didn't want to be associated with her, but Georgia needs to be loved and God has laid it on your heart to love her. Is it really possible to love someone like that?

Man's greatest need is to be loved. We all seek to give it and we all yearn to receive it. Few barriers can resist the mighty force of love, especially God's love. It was God's love that changed the course of history. First-century Christians' love for one another was what set them apart from the rest of the world.

At the time of Christ, hatred was the common practice for Greeks, Romans — and Jews. Racism, caste systems, wars, and prejudice reigned and ruled. So when the followers of Jesus — a sharply diverse group

— demonstrated love to one another, the rest of the world sat up and took notice. Jesus had said, "By this all men will know that you are My disciples, if you have love for one another" (John 13:35). He was right. Onlookers watched and responded in amazement, "Behold how these people love one another!" Soon many of them joined the revolution of love as it swept their world.

The Greek language gives us a better understanding of the meaning of "love." In English we use the same word for various, even unrelated meanings, but Greek is much more specific.

Eros is a word meaning love, but it actually speaks of sensual desire; it is not used in the new Testament.

Phileo, a second word for love refers to the kind of love found between friends or relatives, and conveys a sense of loving someone because he is worthy of our love.

Agape is the third, and purest kind of love. It is used to describe the love God has for us. It is not expressed merely through emotions but is often an act of the will. It is God's supernatural love for us revealed supremely through our Lord's death on the cross in our place. It is the Godlike love He longs to reproduce in us and through us to others, and its source is the Holy Spirit.

Agape is love based on the character of the person doing the loving. It's not dependent on whether the subject of the love is worthy. Sometimes it is love "in spite of," but never love "because of."

A New Commandment

The Lord Jesus gave His disciples a new commandment which applies to us today. He said, "Love each other just as much as I love you" (John 13:34, TLB). But what kind of love was He referring to? To answer that we must explore the kind of love with which He has loved us.

God's love was expressed through His only Son, Jesus, "that whoever believes in Him should not perish, but have eternal life" (John 3:16). It is the very same love that kept the Son of God hanging on the cross in our place to die for our sins. It is the divine, supernatural, unconditional love that God makes available to believers with the command that we are to love one another.

Is it possible that you and I can love with Godlike love? Had the day of Pentecost not occurred, God's love would never have been duplicated in human form. But with the outpouring of the Holy Spirit the disciples found themselves able to love each other as Jesus had. They even miraculously came to love their enemies, the angry mobs who had crucified their Lord. The very people who threatened their lives were seen in a new light.

That love, that *agape love*, is available to us today. It is not an emotional experience but a divine, supernatural power that originates with the Father. This kind of love flows through the Holy Spirit to us, and on through us to those in the world around us. This is what makes it possible for us to love someone like Georgia.

As we acquire God's love within us and learn to incorporate His loving ability into our lives, there are several things we need to know about this powerful love that is ours.

God loves us with UNCONDITIONAL LOVE! We are loved *because of Him, not because of us.* His love for us is never based on our performance. He loves us *in spite* of our disobedience, weakness, sin and selfishness. His love is so great that He chose to love us, even to *die* for us *while we were still sinners* (Romans 5:8). His love is unconditional and completely undeserved.

We are commanded to love. A wealthy, successful young lawyer from the Sanhedrin once approached Jesus with a question his own quick, trained mind could not answer. "Sir," he said, "which is the most important command in the law of Moses?" Jesus answered without hesitation. "Love the Lord your God with all your heart, and with all your soul and with all your mind," He said. "This is the great and foremost commandment." The second greatest commandment? Jesus chose, "Love your neighbor as yourself" (Matthew 22:36-40).

Every other commandment, every other law given by God or designed by man, finds its roots in one of these two which Jesus said were the most important of all. Keep these two laws and you are fulfilling them all. And then Jesus added His own, "This I command you, that you love one another" (John 15:17).

Our Own Efforts

We cannot love in our own strength. We often refuse to love unlovely people. It is easier to love the "beautiful" people. Or to love those who are good to us, and those who appreciate what we do for them. Why love anyone who is unattractive, or peculiar, or grouchy, or disagreeable? Or why even try to love those who just don't love us? First, because God says we must. Second, He provides the strength to obey His every command. In ourselves we have neither the power nor the motivation to love the unlovely, and the Bible explains why: "The old sinful nature within us is against God. It never did obey God's laws, and it never will" (Romans 8:7, TLB).

We cannot demonstrate *agape love*, God's unconditional love for others, through our own efforts. We can resolve over and over to love someone who gets on our nerves and within a matter of days (if it takes that long) we fall right back into our old patterns of avoidance and procrastination, or whatever we are best at. By nature we are too proud to "stoop" to such lowly measures and attempt to love someone who does not love us in return or even appreciate our efforts on his behalf. Our pettiness and jealousies, our pride and selfishness block our path to obedience. It's humanly impossible to love others the way Jesus tells us to love.

With God's Love

But with God in our lives, and through the empowering of the Holy Spirit, God enables us to be different from what we are naturally. He provides the motivation we lack, the ability to love, the creativity to show our God-love. It is a new kind of love altogether.

We can love with God's love. It was God's kind of love that brought us to Christ. It is this same love that sustains and encourages us each day. It empowers us to minister to fellow believers as we have been commanded. This is the same love that brings others to a saving knowledge of Jesus Christ.

But how do we get God's love into our lives? It and the Holy Spirit are inseparable; when we receive Him, we receive His love. Scripture reminds us, "We feel this warm love everywhere within us because God has given us the Holy Spirit to fill our hearts with His love" (Romans 5:5, TLB). God is a Spirit and the fruit of the Spirit is love (Galatians 5:22). When we are controlled by the Spirit we are filled with His love.

And so we are filled with God's love and ready to love the world with this remarkable, unconditional, boundless love. But can we make this love a practical reality in our lives? How will others ever know they are loved if we cannot show them?

Love by Faith

We Love by FAITH. Everything about the Christian life is based on faith; nothing we have received from God has come to us except through faith. We love by faith just as we received our salvation — by faith. We love by faith just as we walk by faith. We love by faith just as we are filled with the Holy Spirit.

Is there a limit? Yes. After we are able to love others as much as Jesus loves us, we can stop. It is God's will for us to love each other, and He does not command us to do anything that He will not enable us to do. We are reminded in 1 John 5:14,15 that anything we ask according to His will He hears and answers. Do you want to love with God's love? Simply claim His promise as it relates to His command to love, and take it by faith.

A fellow worker and I had had a disagreement. I was finding it extremely difficult to work with him. I wanted to love him, and I knew that I was commanded to do so; yet, it was more than I could do. I could not generate the love I needed for this person. And then I was reminded of 1 Peter 5:7 where I am told to cast my anxiety on God because He cares. In obedience I gave the problem and my inability to solve it back to God, and claimed His love for this man by faith. The troubled feelings I had harbored in my heart were gone the moment I considered the problems in God's capable hands.

Within a few hours someone slipped a note under my door. To my surprise it was an unexpected letter of apology from this man I had disagreed with. Without knowing about my decision to love him he too had decided that love was the answer. We met for coffee and prayer, and the fellowship we shared that afternoon was warmer and more rewarding than any we had ever shared.

Love Yourself

Make a list of the people you don't like and claim the promise of 1 John 5:14,15. And begin *now* to love them by faith in this promise from God.

Do you love yourself? Perhaps you will find your own name on your list. The truths of 1 Corinthians 13 (entire chapter) apply to ourselves as well, and can be claimed for ourselves by faith the same as we would claim them for anyone else. Ask God to give you His eyes so that you can see yourself as He sees you. Jesus loves you without reservation, unconditionally. He loves you so much that he died for you while you were still in sin, unaware of your need for His forgiveness. If He — God Himself — can love you that much, who are you to disagree?

Pray for each person on your list, asking the Holy Spirit to fill you with God's love for every one of them. The next time you meet or talk to someone on your list, draw upon His limitless, inexhaustible, overwhelming love for them as an act of faith. Expect God to work through you by faith. Expect Him to use your smile, your gentle words, your patience to express His love to them.

Try this love on each "enemy" in your life — everyone who angers you or ignores you, or bores you, or belittles you, every frustrating human being you know. Then wait to see the results. Men and women around us are just waiting, longing to be loved with God's irresistible love.

The road home seemed longer than usual that rainy April night. The man at the steering wheel had just learned about God's command to love unconditionally as God Himself loves His children. And now, with the windshield wipers beating out a steady cadence he could not shake the picture of his own son.

It had been a foolish argument over . . . funny, he could not even recall what they had argued about, but Wayne had stomped from the house and he had not heard from him since. It had been months now, and he did not know whether his boy was dead or alive. The knot of longing in his middle was growing. "Oh, God," he cried out into the darkness, "I won't believe that Wayne is dead. You know I need to make things right with him. In spite of everything, I want to tell him that I love him." Tears pushed their way down his cheeks and disappeared into his greying beard. "Please, Father," he whispered hoarsely, "let me tell my son how much I love him."

He turned the corner and glanced at the house. Could he be seeing things? The light in Wayne's room was on. It could only mean that the boy was back. Leaving the car in the driveway he rushed through a downpour into the house. "Wayne," he called. "Son, is that you?"

Into the early hours of the morning the father and son talked. "I was so scared to come home, Dad," the boy said. "You have every right to hate me."

"I don't hate you, son," the father said. "God and I love you . . . just the way you are." The father and son embraced. "We're going to make it; you, me . . . and God."

How exciting to have such a dynamic joyful force available to us! And it all comes from our loving Savior, Jesus Christ. He promises that all we need is available to us in His Word. We need not guess, nor hope, nor wish; we only need to claim His love by faith, right now.

Memorize and claim 1 Corinthians 13 and ask the Lord to cement its truth into your life day by day as you draw, by faith, on the limitless resources of love that are yours through the Holy Spirit. It has changed the lives of millions. Let it change yours by praying the following prayer.

"Lord, who calls Yourself Love, I choose to obey Your command to love like You do. I claim Your promise to enable me to love by faith, and I trust You to empower me with the perfect love of Your Holy Spirit."

RECOMMENDED ASSIGNMENTS
Chapter 8

Reflect: I know that I *should* love others. Even my so-called enemies. But there is this one person in my life who is simply *impossible* . . . what should I do?

Interpret: The poets and songwriters have much to say about love. But there is one love letter that will change your life. The Scriptures record the greatest love story ever told. It is summarized in John 16; outlined in 1 Corinthians 13; commanded in John 13:34; and portrayed throughout the psalms. Notice love's relationship to prayer by meditating on John 17. Look up the word *love* in a concordance and see what a challenging topical study it makes.

Apply: Make a list of those whom you are having difficulty loving as God loves. Hypocrisy creeps in unawares. We put on our politeness mask and pretend everything is O.K. But there is someone in your life right now who is waiting to see your *agape* love in action — without any selfish pretentions. Choose today to pray for each person on your list. Expect to see results.

CHAPTER NINE

HOW TO PRAY

"Mommy," the child asked, "what's prayer?"

"It's two people who love each other talking together — one of them is God, and the other is you."

Prayer is simply communicating with the Father who loves us unconditionally. The well-known "hot line" that connects Washington, D.C., with the Kremlin, offers the President instant, direct communication with the Soviet Union in the event of a national emergency. If we liken it to the communication lines between the believer and God, the sad truth is that our spiritual "hot line" to God's heart sits idle much of the time. We seem to forget the line exists until an emergency or crisis arises to remind us that we are not sufficient unto ourselves.

Who can pray?

Instinctively man knows he should pray, and he does, if only to gods of sticks and stone. Whenever we are faced with tragedy, heartache, sorrow or danger, we acknowledge the need within us to turn to someone greater than ourselves and more powerful than our circumstances. But peril lies in praying ignorantly. When men have prayed to gods of blood, fire and war, they have emerged sadistic, ruthless, and militaristic. Man assimilates the moral character of the object he worships. That applies to the Christian as well.

Scripture points out, "There is one God, and one mediator . . . between God and men, the man Christ Jesus" (1 Timothy 2:5). Jesus said, "I am the way, and the truth, and the life; no one comes to the Father, but through me" (John 14:6). Sound exclusive? That is exactly what Jesus intended, to show us that the way to God is very narrow and our focus needs to be on Him and no one else. He must be our only object of worship, for "with unveiled face beholding as in a mirror the glory of the Lord, [we] are being transformed into the same image" (2 Corinthians 3:18). We worship the one true, holy and loving God, and focusing on Him makes us more like Him every day.

Prayer requires a clean heart. Imagine that we have been invited to tea with the Queen of England. What a flurry of preparation would take place! For days we would shop for just the right outfit for the occasion. We would appear before Her Majesty prepared head to toe with a proper haircut and a speech ready to prevent embarrassing blunders.

God asks only that we bring a clean and open heart into His presence. The beloved psalmist said, "If I regard wickedness in my heart, the Lord will not hear" (Psalm 66:18). Our holy God cannot commune with sin; it is the eternal separator. If we would have God hear our prayers, we must confess any sin in our lives and enter His chambers dressed in robes of purity.

We dare to approach His throne with our petitions and praise only on the authority of His Son, the Lord Jesus Christ. He is our only mediator. On the eve of His crucifixion Jesus said no less than six times, "If you ask Me anything in My name, I will do it" (see John 14:13-16).

To whom do we pray?

Every member of the trinity is involved in our prayers. We pray to the Father in the name of the Son through the ministry of the Holy Spirit. Prayer ushers us into the presence of the King of kings and Lord of lords, and we bow in reverence and awe. But He is our Father and delights in our communication. Because of this we can come before Him confident and relaxed, with joyful hearts and filled with expectancy. God loves us more than any human being ever could.

Why do we pray?

1. *Our prayers bring glory to God.* Although our Lord delights in our praise and requests, the purpose of prayer is to glorify Him. Jesus said, "Whatever you ask in My name, that will I do, that the Father may be glorified in the Son" (John 14:13).

2. *We communicate with God through prayer.* Some think of prayer as a convenient "escape hatch" from trouble, a direct route to getting their way, and a means to manipulate God into meeting their needs. To use prayer this way is like filling a shiny new Cadillac with balloons. Prayer is meant to be so much more.

Prayer is a holy line of communication, instituted and commanded by God for the exclusive use of His precious children. The New Testament is filled with directives about prayer and its role in the Christian walk. "Pray without ceasing," Paul said (1 Thessalonians 5:17); "Keep watching and praying" (Matthew 26:41); "Pray with the spirit" (1 Corinthians 14:15). Prayer is important to God, and vital to us. We cannot grow without it.

3. *Prayer is fellowship between God and His children.* God waits eagerly for us to come to Him in prayer. Longing for fellowship, He created man. His love for us was so perfect, so unquenchable, that in spite of our self-centeredness He gave His only Son to pay the price for sin and open a way for us to come

into His presence. Incredible as it seems, God *wants* our fellowship!

Proverbs tells us that "the prayer of the upright is His delight" (Proverbs 15:8). In our egotistical thoughts, prayer has become something for *us*. Something we do to meet *our* needs. But we are being told here that prayer meets the need *in God*, and that we must spend time with Him because our prayers are gifts we offer to please and delight the Lord we love.

4. *Christ set an example of prayer for us.* When Jesus was here among us prayer was a priority for Him. Even in days filled from morning to nighttime with an impossible, pressured schedule, Jesus found time for prayer. He was dependent upon that fellowship with His Father. He escaped into prayer, and restored His wounded spirit. How much more should we be aware of our own need for prayer?

5. *Prayer brings results.* Praying does change things. Jesus prayed for Lazarus who had died, and God restored a beloved friend to life (John 11:43). Elijah prayed that God would forbid it to rain, and for three and one-half years no rain fell in the land. When he prayed again that God would let it rain, the sky became black with heavy clouds that spilled out on the parched ground (James 5:17,18). There is undeniable power in the prayer of the believer.

6. *Prayer is spiritual nurture for the growing soul.* Talking to God and listening for His response, is part of His design to nurture us as we mature in Him. Just as a small child needs nourishment and love to grow strong physically, we need regular food for our souls if we want to mature spiritually. Now and then a day may slip by when we forget to feed on God's Word or communicate with the Father and there may be no apparent ill effects. But if we continue to deprive ourselves of steady nourishment, we will quickly begin to show the signs of spiritual malnutrition. In times of stress

we'll discover that we have lost the strength to live victorious, fruitful lives.

When should we pray?

We are told to *pray without ceasing*, to talk to God about everything, to shoot "arrow prayers" in His direction as we go through the day. We ask for wisdom in difficult places. We thank Him for blessings as they occur. We pray for the salvation of loved ones, and the healing of the sick. We pray for wisdom for our leaders, for our pastors and politicians. And all of this is done as life unfolds around us, on the freeway, in the kitchen with children hanging on our knees, walking through the office.

But there is also a need for *time alone* in a set-apart place where we can kneel undisturbed before an open Bible and talk peacefully with God as we read His Word. We hear God's voice through His Word and through the impressions that come as we open our hearts to meditate in His presence.

As you read the Bible, ask the Holy Spirit to make your reading meaningful and uplifting. Pause often to thank God for His loving provisions, to confess the weaknesses in your life as you see them reflected in Scripture, to ask for the boldness and faith the apostles had, and to thank Him for fresh insights into His plan for your life. Invite God to speak to you, then wait to hear His voice.

Group prayer, in the company of other Christians is another vital part of an active prayer life, yet few gatherings are more dull, unattractive and boring than the average prayer meeting. It is a lack of individual preparation that creates the emptiness we feel at times like these. When we spend time with God in private, preparing for our time together, we come already filled with His presence, expecting Him to do great things as we meet together with Him. Without preparation we can only parrot prayers we have patterned after someone else, and there is no heart in what we say.

How exciting it becomes to talk to God as though He were actually present — as indeed, He is. Prayers are heartfelt and spontaneous, directed by the Spirit.

What does prayer consist of?

The basic elements of prayer can be remembered easily by using the word "ACTS" as a reminder: Adoration, Confession, Thanksgiving and Supplication.

Adoration. To adore God is to worship and praise Him, to honor and exalt Him in our hearts and minds. Our prayers should be an expression of complete trust in Him, a confidence that He hears us. Prayer is much more than words. It is the expression of our hearts, open before God.

Reading psalms of praise aloud, and similar portions of Scripture, can greatly enrich our prayer time. Time spent praising God for His goodness will warm the coldest heart.

Confession. For the Christian who seeks fellowship with God, prayer needs to begin with confession on the basis of Psalm 66:18: "If I regard wickedness in my heart, the Lord will not hear." Isaiah 59:2 reminds us, "Your iniquities have made a separation between you and your God, and your sins have hidden His face from you, so that He does not hear." Confessing our sin prepares the heart for thanksgiving and supplication.

If our discipline of prayer begins with worshipful adoration of God, any sin in our lives will be revealed by the Holy Spirit. For as we see God in His holiness and love, we become aware of our own sin and unworthiness. Someone dressed in white who enters a dark coal mine will not know how smudged and dirty he has become until he stands once again in the light. It is the same with sin. Until we expose ourselves to the "light of the world" (Jesus), we cannot see the dark places in our lives.

We always can be totally transparent with God, for He knows us intimately. We have no secrets before

Him. The hairs of our head are numbered, and He knows our thoughts before we think them. We cannot hide behind a facade, or fool God. So we can come in complete freedom and honesty and tell Him exactly how we feel. If you do not feel spiritual, tell Him. If your heart is cold, confess it. If you have been disobedient, confess it and receive His forgiveness and cleansing; be restored to fellowship once again.

True confession is honest, and it involves:
— acknowledging that our sin is wrong and therefore, is grievous to God;

— accepting God's forgiveness for our sins — past, present and future;

— repenting, aligning our attitude with God about our sin. When we change our attitude, the Holy Spirit then helps us to change our actions accordingly.

We can be confident in our confession because 1 John 1:9 promises: "If we confess our sins, He is faithful and righteous to forgive us our sins and to cleanse us from all unrighteousness." Beware of unhealthy extremes of confession that lead to unnecessary introspection. Accept God's forgiveness once and for all for your sin, then concentrate on His love and acceptance of you as His child.

Thanksgiving. There is no better way to demonstrate our faith than to say, "Thank You, God." The writer of Hebrews makes it clear that without faith it is impossible to please the Father (Hebrews 11:6). We are commanded to give thanks for all things because "this is God's will for you in Christ Jesus" (1 Thessalonians 5:18). To fail to give thanks is to disobey God.

If we are filled with God's Holy Spirit and recognize that He controls all things, we can thank Him not only for the blessings of each day, but also for the problems and adversities. When we meditate on the goodness of God, the salvation He has freely given, eternal life in Christ, the chance to serve, health, food, shelter, a free country . . . we are obeying God's command. And praise has a remarkable effect on us. It is invigorating and edifying. It focuses our attention on what we have instead of what we want, and we can see proof that God is at work in us.

But praise involves thanking God for adversity as well. Make a list of every problem, disappointment, and heartache in your life, then begin at the top and thank God for each entry. We are commanded to give thanks in adversity as a demonstration of faith. Expressing our faith pleases God and allows Him to make Himself strong on our behalf. A critical, unbelieving spirit on the other hand, displeases Him and hinders His efforts to bless and enrich our lives and keeps Him from using us for His glory.

Supplication. Paul encourages us, "Be anxious for nothing, but in everything by prayer and supplication with thanksgiving let your requests be made known to God" (Philippians 4:6). To many Christians, prayer is like window-shopping — they spend a great deal of time looking, but they never make a choice to buy. We must know our hearts; we must know what we need and ask God in specific terms, expecting Him to answer.

Supplication includes intercession for others and petition for our own needs.

We should pray daily for our spouses, our children and our parents. We should pray for our neighbors and friends, our pastor and missionaries, and for other Christians to whom God has given special responsibility. Pray for those in authority.

Pray especially for the salvation of souls, for a daily opportunity to introduce others to Christ and to the ministry of the Holy Spirit, and for the fulfillment of the Great Commission in our generation. Begin with your campus or your community. Pray for and seek to find one or more Christian friends with whom you can establish prayer partnerships.

Christians often do not realize the importance of intercession. The apostle Paul continually prayed for his converts (Ephesians 1:15,16), and he also asked them to pray for him (Ephesians 6:19). Every Christian should pray for others and should encourage other Christians to pray for him.

We must pray for ourselves also that our inner man may be renewed and quickened, empowered by the Holy Spirit. We need to tell God about our problems and ask Him for wisdom and guidance. We should ask expectantly for strength to resist temptation, and for the comfort we need when sorrowing. There is nothing too small or too great to bring before the Lord in prayer. What is important to us is important to Him.

Can we pray with confidence? How?

Can we expect answers to our prayers? Scripture says we can if we abide, ask, believe and receive.

Jesus revealed *abiding* as the key to successful prayer, promising, "If you abide in Me, and My words abide in you, ask whatever you wish, and it shall be done for you" (John 15:7). In other words, if our lives are totally yielded to Him with His Word abiding in us so that we know His will, we can ask anything we wish, for our desire is to do His will.

Abiding is simply walking in the Spirit with no unconfessed sin in our lives and being totally available to God. As we pray according to His will, we know He will answer us (1 John 5:14).

To expect answers to our prayers, we must *ask specifically.* James says, "You do not have because you do not ask." He goes on to explain, "You ask and do not receive because you ask with wrong motives, so that you may spend it on your pleasures" (James 4:2,3). The Lord Jesus speaks with the authority of God when he says, "If you ask Me anything in My name, I will do it" (John 14:14).

Jesus promised, "All things you ask in prayer, believing, you shall receive" (Matthew 21:22). *Believing God* is the heart of answered prayer. God does not ask that we have great faith, simply that we believe in a great and trustworthy God. Jesus said, "If you have faith as a mustard seed, you shall say to this mountain, 'Move from here to there,' and it shall move; and nothing shall be impossible to you" (Matthew 17:20).

But faith is not something we can manufacture on our own; it comes from God (Ephesians 2:8,9). The Holy Spirit produces faith in us as we continue to walk in obedience. Faith is like a muscle: If we don't use it, we lose it.

Receive, by faith, the answers to your requests. If we are abiding in Christ and are controlled by the Holy Spirit, if we are praying according to the Word and will of God, we can expect God to answer our prayers, so be prepared to see some action. Imagine that you are receiving the answers you are seeking and begin to thank God for answered prayer!

Even greater things.

As we bow in prayer, we are tapping a source of power that can change the course of history. God's might, power, love, wisdom and grace are available to us if we believe Him and claim His provision. Prayer is the greatest privilege of the Christian experience because it allows us to be in the very presence of God. When we take the promises of God seriously, claiming all we have been promised, there is no limit to what God can do.

If you would like to unleash the full power of prayer in your life, join me in this prayer:

"Father, You said 'I have not because I ask not.' So, right now I am claiming Your promises because I want to live in mighty victory as You have promised that I can, for Your glory. I pray in Your all-powerful name. Amen."

RECOMMENDED ASSIGNMENTS

Chapter 9

Reflect: As I look at my prayer life, I see that it is as varied as my lifestyle. There are more "kinds" of praying than I realized!

* In my time alone with God, my praying is . . .

* In fellowship with brothers and sisters, my praying is . . .

* As I go about my daily affairs, my praying is . . .

* When I pray with another person for a special need, my praying is . . .

Interpret: In this chapter's section, "Why Are We To Pray?" Dr. Bright gives six different reasons to pray. In your notebook or journal, write down these six passages of Scripture which correlate with each one of Dr. Bright's points:

1. John 14:13
2. 1 Thessalonians 5:17
3. Proverbs 15:8

4. Luke 11:1
5. Mark 11:22-25
6. Philippians 4:6,7

For each one jot down an answer to this question:
How does prayer accomplish this?

Apply: Find a psalm which expresses adoration or praise. Write it down on special paper. Put it in a special place. Memorize it! Or, if you have a creative bent, compose a brief psalm/ prayer of adoration, in poetic form. Musicians, compose your own lyrics and musical score!

CHAPTER TEN

HOW TO BE
AN EFFECTIVE MEMBER
OF THE BODY OF CHRIST

Margaret Rhodes is an unusual woman. Though blind, she was not content just being part of her church membership; she wanted more in her life. Margaret stepped beyond the safety and comfort of organized programs and became a part of the evangelistic movement the church was beginning in her community.

Margaret's pastor, Dr. E. V. Hill, is the dynamic, visionary black preacher who pastors Mount Zion Baptist church in south-central Los Angeles. As part of his plan for reaching the city with the gospel, he asked for a committed Christian in each block of homes to act as a representative, praying and planning with other Christians about how to reach their neighbors for Christ. Margaret volunteered and took the training classes at her church. When she surveyed her block, she found seven other believers, and quickly turned them into team members. Prayer meetings at Margaret's became a weekly event.

"It wasn't long," Dr. Hill says, "till all but one man in Margaret's block had committed their lives to Christ." He chuckles as he adds, "And believe me, he was pretty nervous."

This is one church that is making an impact within its community because individual members are willing to leave the status quo behind and become involved in the needs of those around them.

It was an active, vibrant group of believers like this who made a difference in life for my wife, Vonette, and me more than thirty-five years ago.

Both of us had been exposed to the church in our early lives. We even had been baptized. But it took seeing the love of Christ lived out in the lives of dedicated men and women at the First Presbyterian Church of Hollywood to convince us there was more to Christianity than what we had experienced. Our young faith was fostered and nourished through that fellowship. We began discovering a new excitement in living the Christian life.

It is those few who become excited with the Christ of Christianity and what He is doing in people's lives around the world, who are used of God to make a difference where they are. When unbelievers see *Jesus* in the lives of others, they usually want to know more about Him. Most people are hungry for God's love and eagerly respond to the gospel when they understand who Jesus really is and what He has done for them.

The DeMoss Foundation recently discovered something about the spiritual hunger of our nation. Nancy DeMoss, wife of the late Arthur S. DeMoss, a beloved friend and former board member of Campus Crusade for Christ, waged an evangelistic media campaign through the Foundation that reaped results unprecedented in advertising history, secular or Christian. Spot announcements were aired on television, and full page ads were run in national newspapers and magazines offering a free book called *Power for Living*. In the book, the concept of real power for living was presented in the person of Jesus Christ, the all-powerful one. Those interested were asked to phone or write for a free copy of the book, but no one was prepared for the kind of response that resulted.

More than *eleven million people* wrote or called indicating a personal interest in finding the source of power for living. Books were sent to each one. Over one million wrote back to say they had received Christ personally as a result of reading the book. Only God knows how many millions more opened their lives to Him as a result of the campaign.

On any given Sunday, 40 percent of America's adult population — eighty-five million people — are in church. More than one hundred million adults are on membership rolls, and an additional fifty million identify themselves as Christians. The impact of the church in society is felt by everyone, not just by believers. All too often we seem to forget how important and influential the church of our Lord Jesus Christ is in any community — around the world. Unfortunately, many of the people who fill our churches only know *about* Christ. They do not know Him personally.

Their exposure has been much like that of a small boy who was raised in the South. At the entrance to the park in their town stood a fine statue of General Robert E. Lee sitting proudly astride his powerful horse, Traveler. Every day the boy and his father walked past the monument and stopped to look at the statue of the soldier and his horse. The boy's father, proud that the South had produced such a hero in the Civil War, wanted his son to grow up to appreciate his heritage. "Say good morning to General Lee, Son," he would say.

The boy came to look forward to their daily visits to the general, and every time they stopped at the foot of the statue, he would raise his small hand to the hero before him in a somber salute of respect. "Good morning, General Lee," he would say.

For weeks the boy and his father performed their little ritual at the foot of the statue. One day the child paused. "Daddy," he asked curiously, "who's the man sitting on the back of General Lee?"

The boy had been exposed to the general, but who the man actually was and what he had done obviously had not been communicated clearly so that the boy could understand.

Who could say "no" to the Lord Jesus Christ if they really understood who He is and what He has done for them? If only people could see and understand that only God provides the love and forgiveness they are searching for in their lives.

How clearly do we communicate that Good News? As Christians, it is our privilege — and responsibility — to communicate what we know of the Savior, *accurately and emphatically*. We proclaim glibly on bumper stickers, "Jesus is the answer." The truth is that Jesus *is* the answer, whatever the question! The problem lies in our finite inability to communicate the infinite reality of Jesus to the searching heart. In ourselves, we are not able to meet human needs.

In 1983 both houses of Congress and President Ronald Reagan declared that year as the "Year of the Bible". It was my honor and privilege to serve as chairman of that committee. The President, as honorary chairman, was quoted as saying, "Every problem that we face in our society would be solved if the American people would simply obey the Ten Commandments and the Golden Rule." In light of some of the staggering difficulties facing our society, that may come across as an oversimplified generalization.

But when you really think about it, the solution holds merit. Stop and consider with me for a moment its implications. Could the complex, knotted misunderstandings in a marriage on the brink of divorce be reversed if both individuals began treating their partners the way they themselves longed to be treated? Would it affect the lives of those involved in crimes of violence if they begin living their lives in accordance with the teachings of God? What about chemical dependencies, and child abuse? What of desertion, and immorality? And what about racial hatred, and anything else that comes to mind.

The claims of Christ, if truly given root in a life, can and do change these very circumstances in everyday lives of ordinary people. Imagine — if an entire society lived according to God's design for His creation, it would be revolutionized. Society would progressively change from the inside out. It would never be the same again.

It is for this reason we need to be aware of — and responsible for — our calling as believers. As part of the Great Commission, our very lives need to represent Christ to those around us — Christian and non-Christian alike — to woo and win them into the Kingdom, to build His church.

For the past several years, my ministry responsibilities have taken me to scores of countries on every major continent. I've found that most pastors, missionaries, and Christian leaders around the world agree on two things:

1. God is at work in the world *through His Body, the church* in an unprecedented way.
2. The average Christian misses tremendous opportunities for service through the church, simply because he is not equipped to make a difference where he is. Many are not filled and empowered with the Holy Spirit, nor have they been trained to share their faith in Christ.

Effective membership in the Body of Jesus Christ is built on a foundational principle that cannot be overlooked: *Since Christ's church is His Body, every member must surrender to the Head.* For us to be effective in our witness, Christ must be Lord of our lives just as He is Lord of the church. But, He can be Lord only when we are willing to die to self.

The greatest paradox of the Christian life is that we must die before we can live. The apostle Paul refers to this in Galatians 2:20 when he says, "I have been crucified with Christ; and it is no longer I who live, but Christ lives in me; and the life which I now live in the flesh I live by faith in the Son of God, who loved me, and delivered Himself up for me".

An effective member in the Body has made a total, irrevocable commitment of his or her life to the Lord. It is the second most important decision in the believer's life, and the only way to say with Paul, "[I am] Jesus Christ's slave . . . sent out to preach God's Good News" (Romans 1:1, TLB).

As a part of the Body of Christ, how does being under the Lord's headship affect our everyday life? The New Testament responds to that question with three very direct, easy-to-apply answers. Each one is associated easily with a specific disciple whose life best expressed the principle. The individual members of the early church were energized by these basic principles and they took advantage of every opportunity through:

1. witnessing;
2. service; and
3. fellowship.

Witnessing — Peter

Jesus left His disciples with a promise: "You shall receive power when the Holy Spirit has come upon you; and *you shall be my witnesses*" (Acts 1:8, emphasis added). Ever since the Day of Pentecost, the primary purpose of the church — and each member individually — has been to witness. Filled with the Holy Spirit, Peter said, "This Jesus God raised up again, to which we are all witnesses" (Acts 2:32). From that point on in the book of Acts, when we encounter Peter, it is almost always as a witness. Witnessing is *required* of those under the headship of Christ. The Christian who does not regularly share his faith will soon lose his "first love" and ultimately the power and blessing of God.

Nothing pleases the heart of God more than watching His children as they go about the business of spreading the gospel, then discipling men and women of all nations in Christ. It is the active fulfillment of the Great Commission, and the church suffers most deeply when Christians begin to prefer to be fed, rather than to pour themselves into the lives of others. And the fact remains that without winning, building, and sending those around us, there soon would be no one to carry the Good News.

The writer of Hebrews could have been addressing the many apathetic Christians in the church today when he wrote, "You have been Christians a long time now, and you ought to be teaching others, but instead you have dropped back to the place where you need someone to teach you all over again the very first principles in God's Word. You are like babies who can drink only milk, not old enough for solid food" (Hebrews 5:12,13, TLB).

The question presents itself: With such widespread apathy within the Body, is it possible that an individual can make a difference? The answer is a resounding YES! There are many things individuals can do to keep from being pulled under by apathetic surroundings.

Here are some ideas to get you started:

— Volunteer for evangelistic visitation with your church, then lovingly foster new converts. Channel them into the church, and help establish them in discipleship programs where they can grow into effective witnesses of their faith.

— Where no discipleship program exists, volunteer to begin one. Work with your pastor to locate reliable instruction, then recruit, organize and train others to continue the ministry. Training trainers is what keeps the cycle going.

— Find people who want to grow in Christ and help them find a place of service in the church.

Meet with them once or twice a week for prayer, instruction in evangelism, and discipleship.

— Organize and/or participate in coffees, luncheons, Bible studies, and other events focused on evangelizing non-Christians.

— Work with your pastor, deacons, and elders to contribute not only to the making of disciples, but to the growth of the Body as it is expressed locally.

God will multiply believers through us if we are filled with the Holy Spirit. Many Christians become discouraged in witnessing because their efforts seem to be in vain, despite the fact that they are using the latest witnessing techniques, and are up-to-date on all the new methods. Even the best tools cannot ensure results. We can only be effective witnesses when we are filled with the *only* power source — the Holy Spirit. In ourselves we are powerless. To follow Christ and be filled with His Spirit is to be a productive fisher of men.

Service — Paul

The Book of Acts records Paul's consuming passion for leading men and women to Christ, and discipling them in their faith. And yet, his letters to the churches of the first century have a dominant theme of *service*: "Have this attitude in yourselves which was also in Christ Jesus, who, although He existed in the form of God, did not regard equality with God a thing to be grasped, but emptied Himself, taking the form of a bond-servant" (Philippians 2:5-7). As servants under the headship of Christ we are to give generously of all we are. God promises ". . . whatever a man sows, this he will also reap" (Galatians 6:7).

Jesus spent His life giving Himself to those in need. As His servants we must ask: If Jesus gave His time, money and Himself to others, how can we do less? "A disciple is not above his teacher, nor a slave above his master" (Matthew 10:24).

A servant's heart finds expression in many ways. Henrietta Mears, an influential Christian leader of this century, expressed her servant's heart by being available to those in need. Her door was always open. She once said that she measured her own spiritual commitment by the requests she received from others, feeling that God could use her in others' lives only as she stayed an open channel for His service.

The principle is true for all of us: We can measure our servant's heart by the deeds we do — as individuals and as members of the church. Miss Mears' method was an appropriate expression of her spiritual commitment, not an example to duplicate in our lives. We must each find the method right for *our own* abilities and circumstances by remaining sensitive and responsive to the Spirit of God within our lives.

Service is not a very popular concept in our self-satisfying culture. A subtle attitude of self-centeredness has filtered quietly into the church, and many Christians approach the Body asking, "What's in it for me?" instead of, "What can I give?" Yet the one who strives to be satisfied soon discovers that happiness is elusive. It is the person who lives to give, and who serves others, that reaps true fulfillment and finds meaning in life.

The committed servant gives generously of his wealth. Although we North American Christians comprise only 5 percent of the world population, we possess an estimated 80 percent of the Christian wealth. Untold billions of dollars could be released into the work of Christ around the world if more United States Christians gave with a spirit of generosity.

A servant sees the need of others. Scripture reveals that God has a heart for the homeless, for widows and orphans, the poor, the sick and the imprisoned. His concern for the needy is so strong that Jesus said, "To the extent that you did it to one of these brothers of Mine, even the least of them, you did it to Me" (Matthew 25:40). We need to develop our Christian compassion for the hurting and neglected, the forgotten and afraid in our midst. It is our responsibility as followers of Christ.

A servant spends time on his knees. The power of prayer cannot be overemphasized. It is our communication with God, a vital link to His heart, and a necessary part of the Christian walk that was demonstrated regularly by Jesus as He walked among us. We need to practice the presence of God by taking time throughout each day for quiet moments of fellowship with Him. We need to speak to Him and take time to listen in His presence. We need to bond ourselves to other believers in prayer, through regular times together, praying for personal and local needs, national and worldwide. We need to develop a support system network of prayer around our pastors, praying for them daily, praying with them weekly as their schedules permit.

In the Body we share common duties, but *a servant discovers and uses his unique gifts.* Paul wrote to the church in Rome, "We, who are many, are one body in Christ, and individually members one of another. And since we have gifts that differ according to the grace given to us, let each exercise them accordingly" (Romans 12:5,6). The gift of hospitality gives you a natural means to evangelize non-Christian friends, neighbors and family members. The gift of helps can reach out to the fragmented life of a single parent, or reach into the loneliness of a senior adult, the handicapped, or a wayward child. The gift of encouragement helps disciple young believers.

The disciple's heart longs to be a servant — like the Master. Through it all, the undercurrent of power flows on as we regularly uphold each other in prayer, together or apart. And while we are on our knees before God, we can ask Him for more opportunities to serve.

Fellowship — John

God did not say we would be known as His disciples by our witness, although witnessing is a priority. Neither did He say we would be known as His disciples because of our great acts of service. Instead, He said it would be *our love for one another and our fellowship,* that would link us to Him in the eyes of others. "All men will know that you are My disciples, if you have love for one another" (John 13;35). The greatest power in the world is love.

Luke recorded examples of church fellowship for us in the Book of Acts. When the disciples returned to Jerusalem after Jesus' ascension into heaven, they awaited the fulfillment of His promise together. "These all with one mind were continually devoting themselves to prayer" (Acts 1:14). They shared the anticipation, and the long days of waiting, praying with one another until the promise came.

Then, on the Day of Pentecost, the promise was fulfilled and their fellowship changed dramatically. Where it once had been solemn and exclusive, it now became joyful, and they widened their small circle to include others. The Scripture says, "They were continually devoting themselves to the apostles' teaching and to fellowship. . . . breaking bread . . . taking their meals together with gladness and sincerity of heart. . . . And the Lord was adding to their number day by day those who were being saved" (Acts 2:42-47).

Through the Holy Spirit, we in the twentieth century can share the same kind of fellowship the disciples enjoyed in the first century. In his first letter, John expressed the nature and purpose of our fellowship when he wrote, "We are telling you about what we ourselves have actually seen and heard, so that you may share the fellowship and the joys we have with the Father and with Jesus Christ his Son" (1 John 1:3, TLB).

Members of An Institution or Part of A Movement?

In order to be an effective member of the Body of Christ, we must participate fully in all three of these aspects of the life of the Body: *sharing the gospel, sharing our gifts in service and sharing our life in fellowship.* It is not enough merely to be members of a local institution. We must be part of the movement of God through the church.

Dr. E. V. Hill believes, "Every church member should have a personal ministry to share the gospel with others. The emphasis at our church is more ·on building disciples than enrollment."

Church membership rolls never tell the true story. We cannot be content just to fill the pews on Sunday mornings. To make a difference in this world, we must become a vital part of our churches through our witness, our service and our fellowship together. We must work with our pastors in helping our churches — the Body of Christ — become all they can be, to the glory of God.

RECOMMENDED ASSIGNMENTS

Chapter 10

Reflect: That question at the end of this chapter is a good one: Am I member of an institution or part of a movement? Others may be content with apathy, but I'm not! I want to be dynamic . . . living on the cutting edge. Vital. God, I really want to become a vital part of my church.

Interpret: Romans 12 and Ephesians 4:1-16 are key passages dealing with the Body Life concept. Unity is the goal, but each of us is responsible to discover our unique functions. Search the Scriptures. Instead of searching for self-fulfillment, discover your spiritual gift and start serving others.

Apply: Do you have a servant's heart? Go back to Dr. Bright's list of ideas on pages 113 and 114. Choose one that you can prayerfully implement in the coming weeks. Sharing Christ and discipling others is just the adventure you've been waiting for!